Remodelista

A
Manual
for the
Considered
Home

ARTISAN
NEW YORK

Julie Carlson

With the editors of **REMODELISTA**

Written and edited by MARGOT GURALNICK
Photographs by MATTHEW WILLIAMS

Contents

Foreword

The Internet changed everything for me. In my pre-Google days, I found my design sources by tramping through neighborhoods trolling thrift shops and hardware stores, tearing pages out of design magazines and scouring the resource sections, and inviting myself into the homes of those whose taste I admired. Oh, and by sneaking into showrooms designated "to the trade only"! My results weren't bad, but my methods were hardly efficient.

But suddenly there was the Internet. And I was renovating a house in Montauk. I wasn't even calling it a renovation—I just wanted to "clean it up" inexpensively and quickly, so my family could move in the following summer. I decided I would source everything myself and have it sent out to my contractor, Eddie Eurell, piece by piece. He would call me every morning at 9:30 to give me a progress report and tell me what they were ready to install. And I spent every spare moment on the Internet sourcing light fixtures, faucets, and cabinet pulls. It feels great to discover a plumbing site that stocks most pieces and can overnight them to you, but it is mind-numbing to plow through eighty-one pages of really unattractive extralong bathtub fillers, only to find out that the one you like is the sole piece custom-made in Italy. And has a twelve-week lead time. So when I Googled "outdoor lighting" and a page popped up that said: "10 Easy Pieces: Outdoor Lighting," I couldn't believe my luck. I liked them all! Someone had edited out all the ugly stuff and had chosen ten lovely and easily obtainable outdoor lights. So I ordered some. Boom.

That was my introduction to Remodelista. Upon further exploration (daily on my part), the website proved to be a beautifully designed and curated collection of images, sources, and information about decoration and remodeling, my most passionate avocation. The features are fascinating and useful—"10 Easy Pieces," "Architect Visit," the ever-popular

"Steal This Look." (I admit I felt a huge surge of pride when I found my own house in the "Steal This Look" section.) I had a hard time understanding how four women unknown to me so often shared my taste. Did I know them? Maybe I did! I developed an enormous curiosity about this Julie and this Francesca and Sarah and Christine—how did they manage this? Where did they find their sources? Where do they find the *time*? Why do we all like the same stuff? But at the end of the day, I ceased wondering and just availed myself of their expertise and their generosity.

After I completed my Montauk "cleanup," I continued to frequent the website for purposes of education and entertainment, and when I renovated my Manhattan town house for the *second* time, it was Remodelista I turned to when I needed to very quickly choose several shades of white paint —"Architect's Favorite White Paint," not the five-pound Benjamin Moore paint wheel. What a relief. I now have two new very interesting doormats ("10 Easy Pieces: Doormats") from Commune, and I didn't have to troll every hardware store in lower Manhattan to find them. And when I worked in Toronto last summer, I shopped at the coolest Scandinavian/ Japanese store ever, Mjölk ("City Guide: Toronto"), and finally found flatware that I liked. And before I knew it, I realized that Remodelista had become the first source for me; the first place I turn for information, ideas, and, sometimes, even direction.

Anyway, Julie, Francesca, Sarah, and Christine—thank you. Thank you for the help. Thank you for the website. Thank you for now putting out a book of resources, inspiration, and advice for all of us. And it turns out that I don't know you, but with all that you've shared with me… I kind of *feel* like I do. **—Julianne Moore**

Introduction

Look around you. If you're at home, chances are you see room for improvement. You're not alone. Empowered by the DIY movement and the increasing accessibility of good design, we've all become curators of our domains. The rule-driven, to-the-trade-only approach to home design has flown out the window. In its place, the personal and the meaningful rule the roost.

With this democratization of design, however, the possibilities (and the choices) are endless. Literally. The average kitchen remodel requires 2,500 decisions. And therein lies the hitch. Whether you're a professional or a novice, and whether you live in a closet or a château, the question remains: exactly how do you track down what you love and can afford, and how do you corral it with confidence at home?

Six years ago, we launched Remodelista.com as an answer to that question, creating a digital guide to the home design process. Having survived more than a dozen remodels (thanks to midnight phone consultations and rapid-fire e-mail debates about the merits of one drawer pull over another), our four founding editors decided to pool their resources. Our thinking went like this: why go looking for the perfect faucet or sofa or front hall mirror if your style-savvy neighbor has already found The One? Remodelista is that neighbor, with all the information you'll need cataloged and documented. Who has the interest—and stamina—to spend months tracking down the world's best light switch covers? We do.

And who are we? We're a group of far-flung friends who share a pared-down aesthetic—what we like to think of as a collective design DNA—and a near-obsessive interest in the details. It adds up to a desire to live well and thoughtfully. We research every major (and minor!) purchase to the ends of the earth. And we're never quite finished. We're continually fiddling with our quarters and seeing what the design world is up to. We hope our book inspires you—and that you apply its can-do spirit to your own rooms the way you see fit. We have made it our mission to demystify home design on all fronts, whether you're contemplating a complete overhaul; updating a corner of your living room; browsing for easy, affordable upgrades; or simply looking for a design fix.

This is our start-to-finish field guide to creating your own domestic sanctuary. Use it as both a starting point (flag the looks that speak to you) and a go-to resource when questions arise—as they will—about paint colors, furniture arrangements, and whether it's time to upgrade the kitchen. This book is a companion to our site, but it's not a recap—two years in the making, it features original photographs taken by the talented Matthew Williams expressly for the book, and 95 percent never-before-seen houses, rooms, and design ideas (though avid Remodelista readers will be glad to discover that all-new shots of the founding editors' houses are included).

Living the Remodelista life needn't be expensive or involve outside experts. It also needn't require grandeur of any sort. It's all about training your eye and finding what's right for you. So join us, and make yourself at home.

The Remodelista Manifesto

We prefer the personal to the perfect, and when it comes to design, we're broad-minded, antirules, pro-improvising, and all about mixing things up: Eames meets Etsy. That said, we do have a few firmly held beliefs:

01

Classic and livable trumps trendy and transient.

02

Ikea mingles well with antiques: a mix of high and low animates a space—and allows room for all budgets.

03

Clutter is the enemy. For a sense of well-being, edit out the extraneous.

04

Thoughtfully designed and produced goods made with sustainable materials are a far better investment than big-box bargains.

05

Ordinary utilitarian items,
such as wastebaskets and scrub
brushes, can—and should—be
as pleasingly elegant as center-
of-attention pieces.

06

A room full of neutrals needs
a disciplined dose of color.
Think throw pillows, textiles,
ceramics, and artwork in
vibrant shades.

07

Yin wants yang: masculine
and feminine elements mix
well and benefit from each
other. Add too much of one or
the other and your space will
feel unbalanced.

08

Beauty needn't come at the cost
of comfort or utility. Steer clear
of unwelcoming furniture and
fixtures that don't do their job.

09

A mix of textures makes a
room interesting. Mohair
throws, potted ferns,
velvet upholstery, yes; stray
dog hairs, no.

10

Stay true: live with what
you love.

Twelve Houses We Love

(AND WHY THEY WORK)

Come with us on a tour of a dozen of our favorite dwellings, renovated (and, in two cases, built from the ground up) by their style-savvy owners. We'll decode their design secrets and explain how you can pull off the look.

Remodelista Headquarters

When my husband, Josh Groves, and I bought our house, it was a charmless 1970s builder's special. Working with architect Jerome Buttrick, we gave it new windows, white walls, a high/low mix of furnishings, and a well-planned simplicity.

ABOVE: Remodelista started as a cottage industry—and Josh and I still attend to business from our living room sofa.

OPPOSITE: One of the biggest benefits of our top-to-bottom remodel is tailor-built cabinetry. The living room shelves are detailed with large niches lined in black laminate for holding baskets of firewood and magazines. The upper tiers exhibit my predilection for shiny things.

Who says it's not a good idea to do business with friends? I've made a practice (and a career, as it turns out) of collaborating with my nearest and dearest. I remodeled houses in San Diego, Mill Valley, and Wellfleet, Massachusetts, in rapid succession, working with my friend Jerome Buttrick as chief architect. Then, a few years ago, I launched Remodelista with a trio of pals—Francesca Connolly, Janet Hall, and Sarah Lonsdale. We produced the site from my dining table for three years before my husband, Josh Groves, signed on as publisher (we now operate out of our parent company Say Media's headquarters in San Francisco, but the table is still often put to work).

Before founding Remodelista, I worked as a design writer and editor, but it wasn't until I delved into the remodeling process that I realized how life-changing an experience it is to live in a space of your own making. And how satisfying it is to collaborate with like-minded colleagues. Working in tandem with Jerome (he's a proponent of the clean-lined, the thoughtfully detailed, the artisan-made, and the made-to-be-used, all cornerstones of the Remodelista ethos), Josh and I turned what had been considered a teardown into a lofty, bright, informal family home. What ties our 1,900-square-foot house together, and enables us to live comfortably in close quarters with our two teenagers, is stealth storage. In every room, drawers, cabinets, shelves, and niches, all in the same design language, introduce craftsman detailing and practicality. There's a place for paper towels, mixing bowls, firewood, out-of-season clothes, and cell phone chargers.

Living in a small space means using what you've got. Instead of leading to an entry, our front door opens into the living room (with a coat closet, courtesy of Jerome). Our kitchen is on the tight side. And as the furniture arrangement evolved, a sofa migrated comfortably to right in front of the French doors. That's all part of the casual quality of the house—things don't have to fit exactly so. And yet it's no coincidence that it all works. This is the lab where we at Remodelista practice what we preach.

Spend Here, Save There
A sofa by French designer Catherine Memmi with chartreuse pillows from Merci, in Paris, stands alongside an ad-hoc cinder-block coffee table.

A True Living Room

The key to the house's success is its 20-by-30-foot great room, which Jerome reworked by raising the rafters several feet ("They had been hovering uncomfortably low; it was like giving the place a haircut," he says) and inserting custom-made French doors and transom windows that bring in the outdoors and add a constantly shifting "glowiness"—Jerome is convinced it's the quality of light that makes the space so nice to be in.

02

01 Remodelista Was Launched Here

Meetings, as well as meals, take place around the 10-foot-long dining table, which originally served as Remodelista's communal office space. A Belgian design, it exemplifies my belief in living with less and saving up for what you love (or waiting until it goes on sale). I first admired the table at Summer House in Mill Valley, but held off: too expensive. Years later, when I spotted it at a warehouse sale—marked down from $4,500 to $600—I swooped in. The Cape Cod landscape painting is by family friend Robert DuToit.

02 A Clear Division of Labor

Jerome separated the dining area from the kitchen by introducing a genius two-sided partition—it has a tall bookcase on one side and a sink, counter, and low cabinets on the other—that allows a free flow of conversation between people in the two rooms. It's made of ApplePly, a marine-grade maple plywood, with edges exposed; the laminations create a subtle geometric pattern.

03

03 A Kitchen Designed for Action

Dinnertime drop-ins are a frequent occurrence—and I love to cook—so it was important that the simple horseshoe kitchen be kitted out for action. In such tight quarters, well-designed storage allows all the necessities to be kept on hand but, mercifully, out of sight. "Every time you see a nook or cranny," says Jerome, "it's worth thinking about what could go there." The most eye-catching detail in the kitchen is the open shelving for mixing bowls. Jerome also devised wooden niches above the sink for a roll of paper towels and everyday glasses.

04 The Landing Pad

A cubist sculpture of sorts inserted alongside the fridge—the "concierge desk," as I call it—is a good-looking answer to a universal question: where to stash the cookbooks, the electronics, and the old-fashioned phone? For me, it's a much-used workstation that enables me to watch a pot while also editing a post and chatting with a Remodelista colleague.

05 Lab Parts

The black counter material is Richlite, a durable, warm-to-the-touch paper resin that was used in the living room to frame the fireplace. Also direct from a laboratory: my Chicago faucet from the Sink Factory in Berkeley, which specializes in assembling customizable Chicago parts. I find its straightforward design so satisfying that I used Chicago fixtures in every space in the house that involves water.

04

05

06 Under-the-Stairs Gallery

In an unused space below the open-rise steel-and-oak stair that leads to a newly built master suite, I came up with the idea of creating a display space for family photos and art. The aluminum shelving supports are from Rakks, a favorite source with architects; my contractor made the painted shelves.

07-08 A New Spin on the Laundry Room

Using the same maple plywood that's in the living room and kitchen, Jerome fit the laundry room into a hallway outside the downstairs bathroom. Behind a clean-lined jigsaw puzzle of cabinetry, there's a stacked washer and dryer, a linen cupboard, pullout hampers, a shelf for ironing and folding, and drawers for essentials like batteries, lightbulbs, and cleaning supplies. Though I'm not exactly a fan of doing laundry, this setup is one of the most satisfying parts of our house.

Twelve Houses We Love

09

09   Light from Above

The bathroom is dappled with sun that filters in through a museum-style slatted skylight—a sculptural and more diffuse alternative to the standard hole-in-the-roof skylight. Carrying on the clean white look, the ceiling is hung with lights from Rejuvenation (see "The Remodelista 100," page 331).

10   A Combination Dressing Room and Bathroom

The tall, narrow bathroom has a layout foreign enough to require subtitles. The shower and bathtub are located outside the glass door on a deck (because deck space didn't count in the addition's overall square footage—and who doesn't love bathing outside?). That design decision freed up the bathroom itself for not just a sink (Cesame, with a custom steel base) and a toilet, but also for cupboards, closets, and, as in the kitchen, a row of niches, which I fill with baskets of out-of-season clothes. Note that it's the fact that the bathroom is largely moisture-free that allows for so much clothing storage.

10

Master Bedroom Aerie

While the downstairs is dedicated to kids, guests, and work, upstairs Josh and I carved out our own catbird seat overlooking the treetops. Because of complicated building restrictions, every inch of the upstairs had to be masterfully planned. The bedroom is a mere 300 square feet, but it feels bigger thanks to its peaked ceiling.

Steal This Look

02
Convincingly Real Fakes

For me, practicality trumps preciousness: when keeping the tall kitchen counter vase filled with olive branches began to feel like a full-time job, I gave in to real-looking fakes. The look-alikes are from EarthFlora.com, specialists in "alternative foliage."

01
Smart Stove Accessories

The pot-filler faucet over the stove is one of our best remodeling decisions; we use it constantly for filling pasta pots and the teakettle. Available for about $200, it's made by Chicago Faucets.

03
Shaker Peg Display

In our bedroom, where storage is sparse, I use a Shaker Workshop pegboard to hold bags, scarves (on a Japanese wire hanger), and a favorite blouse. But more than storage, the display supplies a shiftable dash of visual excitement to an otherwise quiet space (see "The Remodelista 100," page 300, for more on Shaker peg systems).

05
High/Low Doorknobs

In the public area of the house, we sprang for Baldwin egg-shaped Estate doorknobs in satin-finished chrome (top) that go for about $200 each. Elsewhere, we economized by using similar but more basic Schlage doorknobs (above), which you can find online for $20.

04
A Life-Changing Medicine Cabinet

Designed to match the steel base of the master bathroom sink, our custom medicine cabinet was a $500 splurge that, to our surprise, has more than earned its keep. Its satisfyingly simple detailing is worth replicating. Note the slim vertical bar on the edge of the frame that serves as the handle and the built-in slot (with outlet) for an electric toothbrush. If we ever move, we're carving it out of the wall and taking it with us.

French Bohemian in Fort Greene

Designer Corinne Gilbert's apartment is a lesson in what she calls "improvising in a rental." It's also the essence of casual French style—and filled with ideas for the taking.

ABOVE: Corinne in her dining room. She designs by intuition and has a knack for the unorthodox mix.

OPPOSITE: In Corinne's dining room, a table and lamp of her own design are surrounded by an odd lot of chairs. Though she tried a matched set, she found she preferred living with a cast of characters. Note the overhead light made from a clip-on lampshade.

Picture a fringed mohair throw tossed over an old-fashioned steam radiator with a leather basket balanced on top. Sloppy? Hazardous? Not necessarily. Corinne Gilbert's off-the-cuff design solutions—including making use of a cast-iron heater as storage in the warm months—come off as rakishly elegant and practical. A Paris native with a degree in French literature from the Sorbonne, she's a fashion designer and a Belgian-trained decorative-finishes painter who now focuses on interiors. With her business partner, artist Dan McCarthy, she runs MC & Co., a Brooklyn firm that designs artisanal objects for the home, such as irregularly shaped oval wall mirrors edged in Day-Glo colors and lamps with shades made from men's striped shirt fabric screen-printed with dots.

Corinne grew up in a strictly modernist Eames household. But she spent a lot of time at her grandmother's place in the Loiret, the French equivalent of the Midwest, where each summer her family, led by her engineer father, set up their own quarters by dragging in things from the attic. "So I oscillate between the minimalist and the homey," she says. The rooms she devises for clients tend to be fully realized, streamlined environments that are all about exquisite materials. But at home in a rental comprising the top two floors of an 1870s unrenovated town house in Fort Greene, Brooklyn, Corinne patches together her rooms like a student: "Everything is somewhat makeshift and temporary." Allow us to add that it's the insouciant quality of the place that gives it so much charm.

Linen and Straw

In a corner of her design studio, Corinne piled a futon bench with pillows in natural linen, old ticking, and a bandanna print from her company, MC & Co. The mirrors and lamps are also MC & Co. designs. The simple backdrop ties together the space. It carries onto the floor, where Corinne uses $20 Chinese straw mats from PearlRiver.com to cover an intricate inlaid-wood floor that, to her, "looked like a cheap cigar box."

01 The Low-Commitment Living Room Sofa

Like so many of us, Corinne fears big expenditures that leave her feeling locked in: "Every time I buy a new sofa I feel a bit trapped. I like to camp out and to constantly switch things around." Here, her solution is a futon that doubles as a guest bed. It's covered in a heavy linen bedspread with pillows of her own design.

02 Wall Jewelry

In an intriguing corner of the dining room, what looks like a beaded necklace for a giant is actually a string of Japanese balsa-wood fishing floats found in a Williamsburg antiques store. It's a look we plan to imitate.

03 Putting Walls to Work, Pinterest-Style

In lieu of a bulletin board, thumbtacked clips and colored tape turn a wall into a living scrapbook.

04 A Home Office Fit for a Card Shark

A 1960s game table by Joe Colombo—purchased from a dealer in Italy and one of the few splurges in the apartment—serves as Corinne's computer station. It has pullout ashtrays at each corner, handy for paper clips. Corinne's drawing board: a rectangle of chalkboard paint that floats like a painting.

05 The Galley Kitchen (with a French Twist)

What to do with the worst room in a rental? The kitchen, much to Corinne's chagrin, retains its sixties-era appliances and Band-Aid-pink Formica. While leaving it be, she's made it her own by using a Basque tablecloth as a curtain and a rectangular tray as a radiator shelf. The black lacquerware that sits on the tray (when the heat is off) forms a cozy vignette with a whale made from metal tools by artist Christopher Come and a Dan McCarthy wall-mounted votive.

06 Wallpaper Table as Homemade Buffet

A collection of vases and art rests on a dining room sideboard assembled using the legs of an old wallpaper table, with a plank of whitewashed wood on top. During dinner parties, it's put to work as a serving table.

A Dialogue Between Objects

A white-framed portrait of Corinne by Dan McCarthy is hung intentionally low, so that it peeks over the back of a butterfly chair. The proximity of the two, their shared whites, and the chair's drapings create a feeling of chumminess, as if these objects had plopped down to catch up with each other.

Literary Fortress

A collection of mostly pale-colored paperbacks mounded atop a mantel lends texture and interest to Corinne's quiet bedroom. She says that the only trick is to use strong bookends and create sturdy-enough piles that you avoid an avalanche. It's also wise to take note of the overall palette as you build.

Steal This Look

01
Patched Seating

When oil spots appeared on a corduroy beanbag chair in the living room, Corinne stitched on patches in white and pale pink canvas, as she often does on pillow covers. It was an undeniable improvement; the piece now looks far more interesting than it did when it was unstained.

02
Tablecloth Curtains

Corinne says she has been making her own quickie window covers from sheets and tablecloths since she had her first apartment: "It's a French thing." She folds over the top of the fabric (only occasionally hemming it) and sews on wooden rings. For shades over windows lacking in views, she simply drapes diaphanous fabric over a tension rod.

03
Metal Radiator Cover

To make the radiator blend with the walls and enlarge the feel of the dining room, Dan McCarthy used a sheet of white-painted steel as a cover. For textural interest, he paired it with a shelf of perforated steel and had the parts welded by a metal shop.

04
The Well-Composed Side Table

Corinne designs instinctively, but there are some underlying laws behind her choices: (1) A limited palette is unifying. (2) Warm textures, such as plaster and leather, are easy on the eyes. (3) To avoid a chaotic look, objects need to be edited and well placed—grouping things together allows them to play off, rather than shout at, one another.

05
Indoor Picnic Table

A table with a white wooden top and sawhorse legs straddles the line between refined and rustic. Corinne salvaged the sawhorses from a construction site at a fancy house and thinks they're made from mahogany, but she notes that any would work. Dan built the top from planks of fir joined on the underside with a few pieces of wood and painted it Benjamin Moore China White in an eggshell finish.

Fully Finnish

At their Hamptons compound, fashion stylist Tiina Laakkonen and tech entrepreneur Jon Rosen redefine Scandinavian modernism and discover the power of wallpaper.

ABOVE: Tiina, viewed through a glass door in the living room, with her cat, Monkey.

OPPOSITE: Arabia ceramics in deep blues pattern the kitchen, which is divided from the dining area by a bleached oak table with a zinc top and bottom shelf. Made for the space, it doubles as a work surface and a breakfast perch (the stools are vintage, restored with woven Danish paper cord).

See Tiina and Jon's bathroom on pages 234–237.

Like many of us, Tiina Laakkonen and Jon Rosen each came up with a vision of the ideal home sometime close to birth. Jon spent formative summers at his family's place in Amagansett, New York. To him, the former de Menil estate in nearby East Hampton, a collection of restored historic houses and barns, represented the height of living. Meanwhile, Tiina was growing up in Finland's industrial southeast, where she was raised on Finnish folklore and aware of, if not exactly surrounded by, modernist design. (Marimekko's creator, Armi Ratia, hailed from a town nearby.)

A former model, Tiina earned her design creds working as an assistant to Karl Lagerfeld at Chanel and as the fashion editor at British *Vogue*. "And then love brought me to New York," she says, referring to her husband, a photographer turned tech entrepreneur. Eventually, the two bought a 1950s house in Amagansett, on a sloped meadow with mature trees and no visible neighbors. Modeled on a potato barn, the structure was in rough shape and deemed not worth saving. That was fine with Jon and Tiina—they had already fully imagined the compound that would take its place: a group of vernacular structures, more de Menil than potato barn. And it would be furnished with what Tiina calls her own "tightly curated version of all things Finnish."

They signed on two young New York architects, Tim Furzer and Nandini Bagchee, each of whom has their own firm, though they frequently collaborate. "We sat around a kitchen table with them, and the place came together," says Jon, who was on site daily during the two years of construction. As that was happening, Tiina was rediscovering her roots. She soon found herself with such a singular collection of Scandinavian design that she decided to go into business. Tiina the Store, in a bungalow on Amagansett's Main Street, is a mini version of Tiina the House. The latter, though long in the planning and expansive—five bedrooms, three and a half baths, and a total of 5,000 square feet—was fully furnished in three days flat. "When you build your own place," explains Tiina, "you ask, 'How do I want to live?' 'What kind of sink do I like? What kind of rugs?' For people like me and Jon, there aren't a million answers."

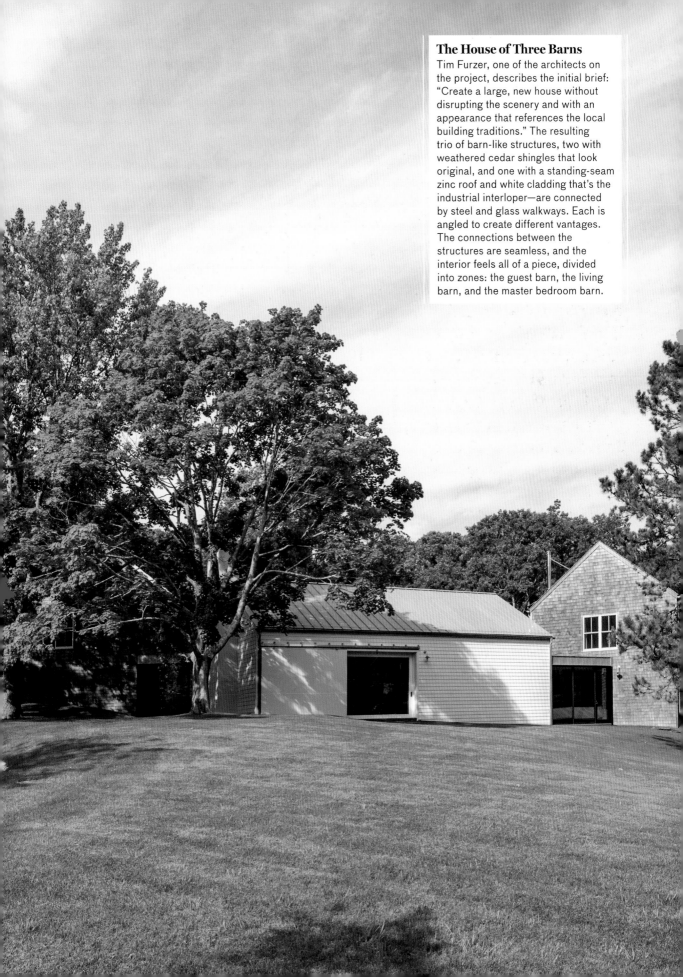

The House of Three Barns

Tim Furzer, one of the architects on the project, describes the initial brief: "Create a large, new house without disrupting the scenery and with an appearance that references the local building traditions." The resulting trio of barn-like structures, two with weathered cedar shingles that look original, and one with a standing-seam zinc roof and white cladding that's the industrial interloper—are connected by steel and glass walkways. Each is angled to create different vantages. The connections between the structures are seamless, and the interior feels all of a piece, divided into zones: the guest barn, the living barn, and the master bedroom barn.

Rusticity of the Highest Order

The entire interior is sheathed with 8-inch-wide poplar shiplap, a tour de force of custom cabinetry that's a sophisticated riff on classic barn walls. The living area overlooks the lush surroundings through two 9-foot-by-12-foot glass doors on stainless-steel tracks recessed into the polished concrete floor. And, in keeping with the country theme, Tiina reupholstered her George Sherlock sofas in a patchwork of early Marimekko prints that establish the house's palette of black, white, and indigo.

01 The Artful Farm Table

Open to the living area and the kitchen, the dining area is set off by a table made from floorboards by Dutch designer Piet Hein Eek, who is celebrated for his line of scrapwood furniture. "Not everyone likes a bench, but I do," says Tiina by way of explaining the table's compromise: a bench on one side and Scandinavian chairs from eBay on the other.

02 Teacup Determinism

A low black marble bench in the dining area displays Tiina's collection of 1940s–1970s rice grain porcelain made by Arabia of Finland, mostly acquired piece by piece over a two-year stretch from private sellers on eBay. She explains: "When I was a kid, my boyfriend's mom had the teacups. I thought they were the most beautiful things and said, 'Someday, I'm going to have them.'"

03 All About Blue

The living area is a show-and-tell of some of Tiina's favorite objects—all in the black, white, and indigo color scheme that crops up throughout: "I'm a one-trick pony. I like doing variations on a theme." The ceramics date from the 1940s and are by Finnish designer Birger Kaipiainen, whose work Tiina calls "the biggest inspiration" in her decorating. The overdyed table is from Moroso's Diesel collection.

Fully Finnish

Twelve Houses We Love

The New-Scandi Kitchen

Tiina sketched the design for the kitchen herself and had it fabricated by St. Charles, a company famous since the 1930s for its powder-coated steel cabinetry: "I wanted it to be purely industrial and functional." And not too big. Bemoaning the scale of American kitchens, she looked to Ikea as her model for European sizing and opted for one of Viking's more diminutive ranges. The point of the custom hood is to have it "not look like a monster. We said, 'Let's build it short and cantilever it out.'"

04 The Secret to an Orderly Front

The refrigerator and microwave are sequestered at the far end of the kitchen in a floor-to-ceiling block of St. Charles stainless-steel cabinetry that calls to mind the Chrysler Building. Opposite it, Tiina tucked a hidden walk-in pantry—"I lived in London, where pantries are a must." It's the dumping ground that enables the rest of the kitchen to look so clutter-free.

05 Beautiful Basics

Tiina likes consistency. Just as her doorknobs and window hardware all have a dark finish, her flatware is black-handled—and classic. A reissue of the 1958 Lion pattern, it's made by Finnish company Hackman, a division of Iittala, and not (yet) for sale in this country.

06 Flight Pattern

A portal to a Scandinavian dreamland: Rut Bryk's butterfly-patterned Apollo wallpaper covers the main wall in the master guest room. Tiina's shop is the lone U.S. source for it and other reissued Finnish midcentury patterns; see TiinaTheStore.com.

07 Wallpaper Comeback

Night of the Skylarks wallpaper puts in a dazzling appearance in the powder room, as well as in several other spots in the house. "If you keep a controlled color scheme, you can do a lot of pattern," says Tiina of the design by Birger Kaipiainen, which dates to the 1950s, when Finland was in the midst of a craft and folklore revival.

Twelve Houses We Love

Daring to Go Dark

Tiina treats wallpaper as art. To maintain mystery and avoid overkill, she typically only covers an interior wall or two, rather than whole rooms. Here, she used Rut Bryk's Apollo design with a black background.

Little House on the Finnish Prairie
A corner of the master bedroom is kitted out with a refined collection of cabin essentials: a cast-iron stove by Danish firm Mørso for cold winter nights, a cast-iron teapot (for humidifying the air when the stove is on), and a woven kindling basket. The inset stove floor is poured concrete. The rug is by Finnish company Tikau.

Steal This Look

02
A Bit of Bright
Decorator Albert Hadley's famous edict that every room needs a pop of red applies even in a house that's all about blue. Here, a desk lamp serves as the equivalent of a sprinkling of salt.

01
Photos in Little Black Frames
Throughout the house, including in Tiina's office (shown here), groupings of photos are framed in black or white. For small images, Tiina uses this trick: "I go to a frame shop and have them make my frames out of frame trim," she says, referring to the narrow border material customarily used for creating small frames within larger ones. "I find it lighter and often more interesting than actual framing."

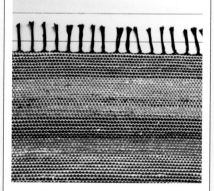

03
Sexy Rag Rugs
Cast aside the frumpy reputation. Against gray-painted wood floors, rag rugs look crisp and arresting. Finnish farmhouse classics, Tiina's rugs are woven by her sister-in-law and available through TiinaTheStore.com.

04
Textile Panel as Curtain

An ideal bathroom curtain allows in sunlight while screening out the world. The beauty of this example: no sewing was required. It's a beloved piece of fabric—made by Dosa from recycled jamdani, a handwoven muslin, appliquéd with patterned jamdani scraps. Clipped to curtain rings, it hangs on a rod from Pottery Barn.

05
Matte Black Hardware

Black knobs add a graphic note to an all-white interior—and cohesion when the same hardware is used throughout. Tiina and Jon's are Nobilus's PK knobs in nickel with a charcoal black finish (their window latches are also Nobilus and chosen to match the doors). Nickel was selected so that when the pieces wear, they'll have a silvery rather than a bronzy look, in keeping with the cool tones of the house. For a lower-priced alternative to Nobilus, see Rejuvenation's Hyde design.

Shaker Redux

In what had been an asbestos-shingled handyman's hideaway, Robert Highsmith and Stefanie Brechbuehler—the founders of upstart architecture firm Workstead—used hardware-store and lumberyard supplies to devise the ultimate in simple style.

ABOVE: Robert and Stefanie in the side yard of their 1850s house, which they freed of its green asbestos shingles.

OPPOSITE: As soon as the place was theirs, the couple took a sledgehammer to the tacked-on front porch, but they kept the steps. In place of a scalloped vinyl door, they introduced a mid-nineteenth-century wooden door intended for an interior. Because it's only an inch thick, their contractor warned them that water could seep in and necessitate floorboard replacement. "Sometimes it's worth ignoring the advice," says Stefanie. "I'd rather see a beautiful door for twenty years."

Seven years ago, a psychic told Stefanie Brechbuehler that she'd marry a Tom Hanks look-alike who would be her partner in life and in work, her "rock." When a former classmate from the Rhode Island School of Design's architecture school made a cross-country road trip to visit her, the prophecy began to take shape. Stefanie is now married to Robert Highsmith, and together they founded Workstead, one of the most talked-about young architecture firms in New York.

To attract their first commissions, they used their own modest rental apartment as a showcase for their approach, which might be described as combining Shaker rigor with a palpable joie de vivre. The place appeared in *The New York Times,* and as hoped, almost overnight, Workstead was in demand, hired to design the lobby and bar of Brooklyn's buzzing Wythe Hotel and to supply their long-armed industrial lighting internationally. "This is really a lifestyle for us," says Stefanie. "We live and breathe what we do."

Robert is a fourth-generation architect who grew up in North Carolina. Stefanie is Swiss; her family moved to the States when she was eight and eventually settled in New Jersey—"My friends say I'm Swiss Jersey." She studied interior design at the Art Institute of Chicago and worked for Michael Graves before going to RISD. She and Robert share a passion for thinking about every detail of their work, down to the door hinges.

The couple got married in a giant Dutch barn in New York's Hudson Valley, and soon started hankering for their own retreat. Things worked out: they now spend four nights a week in Brooklyn and three in the tiny town of Gallatin, where they live in an 1850s farmhand's cottage. Situated on a wooded perch next to a Class A trout stream, the house was moved from its farm locale a few miles away to its present location in the 1940s, which is when the concrete foundation and toothpick front porch came into the picture, followed in the ensuing years by vinyl siding, asbestos shingles, and particleboard paneling. The couple saw their job as "not fussing too much, just peeling back the layers," says Robert. Doing nearly all the labor themselves and relying on local resources for supplies, they remodeled inside and out in a nonstop eight months. Be it ever so humble, their homestead is now a model Workstead design.

A Forest of Woods

The stained oak dining table was found on an antiquing detour in Virginia during a road trip. "At first we were thinking all the wood in the house needed to match the floor," says Robert, "but then we realized that's a mistake. We have lighter wood on the floor, and darker in the furniture." In other words, a mix works. The chairs are 1940s wood folding seats that cost as little as $10 each—the couple collected dozens from eBay and yard sales to use at their wedding.

Camp-Style Living
The house is a mere 950 square feet, and about a quarter of that is devoted to the small living room. Throughout the remodel, Stefanie and Robert camped out on an air mattress amid the sawdust— which, perhaps, explains why they eventually filled the room with campaign furniture: 1950s safari chairs by Danish designer Kaare Klint, wooden folding stools that double as canes, and a coffee table that they made from an old cot (see page 274). The corner wall light is a Workstead design.

01   A Desk Built for Two

Stefanie and Robert spend Thursday to Sunday at the house, so they needed a workspace. Using ready-made turned-wood legs and other parts from Lowe's, Robert built their partners desk in one fruitful afternoon.

02-03   Simplicity Accessorized

Old things are part of the Workstead philosophy. Explains Stefanie: "We try to limit our purchases of new furniture and objects, preferring the story and character of vintage and reconfigured pieces and family hand-me-downs. Most important, we believe in buying things once." Displayed as an art object when not in use, the vintage croquet set was a wedding present. A found-on-the-street pedestal elevates an old electric fan.

04

04 The Reinvented Country Kitchen

The couple planned to demolish the dark, wood-paneled kitchen, but they only got as far as removing the pebble-patterned linoleum flooring before budget and time pressures intervened. Instead, they painted the cabinets, including the metal strap hinges, a Benjamin Moore color match of Farrow & Ball's Lamp Room Gray, and added hardware-store unfinished wood knobs that have a satisfyingly plain and simple look. "We were amazed by how much we could accomplish just by making cosmetic changes," says Stefanie.

05-06 Mixing Period and New Appliances

Robert says they've grown to love the 1960s harvest-gold stove and yellow Formica counters: "They make us laugh, and they're a part of the story of this house." They did, however, replace the dishwasher with a (not entirely reliable) floor model from Home Depot.

Linen Makes a Bed

In the second floor home office, a daybed purchased at a church rummage sale looks both luxurious and completely relaxed. Its high-backed design appeals to Stefanie and Robert because two can read on it, each leaning against an end. The Belgian linen pillows and sheets are by Libeco Home and came from Greenhouse in Brooklyn. "They added up to about a thousand dollars," says Robert, "while the bed was only twenty dollars, so this is definitely one of the high/low moments of the house."

07

08

07 The Tiniest Room
Resuscitated

The dollhouse-sized downstairs powder room was completely transformed by a coat of white paint. "For gloomy spaces such as this," says Stefanie, "white paint is nothing short of miraculous." The couple advocates using top-quality paint, not only for looks but for ease of coverage. Farrow & Ball is at the top of their list, but it's expensive. The white throughout the house is Valspar, a brand they like from Lowe's, in a shade mixed to match a wall chip of the house's original white.

08 The Circle, the Square,
and the Wishbone

In the master bedroom, simple geometrics add up to an eye-pleasing vignette. The hoop, likely from a wagon wheel, was found on the property. The mahogany-framed mirror is from Bad Corner Antiques, in Salisbury, Connecticut. The Hans Wegner Wishbone chair is a Brimfield flea market purchase.

09 The Family Beds

The twin spool beds in the guest room belonged to Robert's grandparents— "You can see the worn spot where my grandmother held the post as she was getting out of bed every morning." The dark wood particleboard paneling on the walls got two coats of white paint, and the beds were up next, but it didn't feel right to Robert: "They're old and worn in a nice way. Painting them seemed sacrilegious."

10 A Four-Poster Trimmed to Fit

The master bedroom is tightly configured, with low windows and a curved ceiling. Ready to swap out their air mattress, the couple found a Shaker four-poster in a local secondhand store. At home, they discovered it didn't fit—until they got out a saw and trimmed the legs and the posts. Now it seems custom-built for the space.

11 A Cure for the Common Accordion Closet

Stefanie and Robert originally planned to replace the bifold hollow-core doors on the guest room closet. Instead, they painted them gray and added the same hardware-store wood knobs used in the kitchen. Done.

Steal This Look

01
Bulb Lights

Like many of Workstead's lighting designs, the kitchen ceiling fixture features a clear-glass globe bulb; made by Bulbrite, they cost about $12 and are available online. ("People think that they're Edison bulbs, but we hate those," says Robert. "They're so obvious.") The porcelain socket is a $3 hardware-store staple officially known as a one-piece keyless porcelain lamp holder. Finding it in black, however, is tricky, so Robert spray paints theirs.

02
Nailed Art

Collages made from Hermès catalogs by artist Brandon Hinman are on view in the dining area. Because the paper is irregularly shaped, Stefanie says that having them custom-framed would have cost hundreds. Instead, she and Robert spent less than $1 and hung them directly on the wall using barely noticeable white ring shank nails (available from hardware stores). For clean, well-positioned holes, they first marked the location of each with a pencil and then punctured the paper with a nail tip before driving the nails through. To make the art more prominent, they floated it away from the wall so that it casts a subtle but detectable shadow.

03

Swapped-in Sofa Legs

Stefanie and Robert are happy with their Ikea Karlstad sofa but couldn't abide its clunky building-block-shaped feet. Luckily, replacing them was as easy as unscrewing the old feet and screwing on new ones (turned maple bun feet found at Lowe's for $6 each). For a well-designed leg collection made expressly for Ikea furniture, check out Swedish company PrettyPegs.se.

04

The Concealed Shower Door

The house's master bath came with several strikes against it, including a prefab shower box and sliding glass door. Until they're able to replace them, Stefanie devised an easy cosmetic fix: she hung a metal tension rod and masked the whole thing behind a hemp shower curtain from Rural Residence in Hudson, New York.

05

Push-Button Lights

Last updated in the 1940s and '50s, the house had rocker light switches and plastic plates. Robert upgraded all of them with push-button switches and brushed nickel plates, both from Rejuvenation, which offers the option of a dimmer that works at the turn of a knob. The switches have an early industrial appeal, like rotary phones but without the extra work, and are easy for an electrician to install. Robert put theirs in himself—"It just involves two wires"—in a matter of minutes.

Zen Industrial

Christina Kim's Asian-inflected fashion and home designs have a cult following. (Count us among the worshippers.) You can see why at Dosa 818, her company's live-work loft.

ABOVE: Christina serves salad in a Heath Ceramics Chez Panisse bowl that's part of the tableware line she designed with Alice Waters.

OPPOSITE: Nearly all of Dosa 818's 6,000 square feet are kept wide open, with restored or rebuilt steel-framed windows all around. When Christina and her longtime architectural collaborator, Lindon Schultz, began work, the space had been abandoned for years and was horribly fire-damaged. Though today it looks convincingly raw, the renovation took four years. "Our dream," says Christina, "was to do something very local using materials recycled from the building and the neighborhood."

Launched in 1986, Christina Kim's fashion label, Dosa, stands out not only for its exquisitely detailed, wabi-sabi simplicity—picture a silk slip dress in the iridescent green of a peacock's feather—but also for the humanity behind it. Her singular approach is, as the *Los Angeles Times* has described it, to encourage people "to consume less but cherish more the things they buy and wear, including the sweat equity and consummate craftsmanship of the people who made them." Born in Seoul, South Korea, and trained as an artist, Christina frequently works with craft collectives in distant corners of the world, helping to keep indigenous techniques alive and vital.

A love of everyday objects led her to branch out into housewares. Twice a year, she presents a small, compelling collection: towels of hand-spun and hand-loomed Indian khadi cotton, Turkish filikili rugs in shades of fuchsia and platinum, and Moroccan-style metallic leather poufs filled with polar fleece remnants. Of late, none of the scraps from Dosa's clothing production go to waste—they're turned into yardage or appliqués or patchwork totes or pouf stuffing. Christina has also made a mission of using natural and environmentally acceptable materials and dyes. By example, she has shown that it's possible to be low-impact *and* high-fashion—and that applies to Dosa's work environment as well.

Occupying the penthouse of the art deco Wurlitzer Building in downtown LA, Dosa 818 is a temple-like loft that's a combination Dosa flagship store, art gallery, and idea lab, curated—down to the fuzzy orange kitchen sponge—by Christina. After hours, 818 becomes a crash pad for out-of-town business associates and friends (as it was for Christina recently while she completed the renovation of her house). In a space she describes as "big enough to accommodate both contemplation and cartwheels," she has fashioned not just a remarkable business but also a new way of life.

01 Christina's World

Christina surrounds herself with totemic objects. On a bench, incense burners (the large one is a prehistoric relic given to her as a present; the small one is from Kathmandu) stand next to a charm necklace of sorts. Made from a Japanese shoestring, it holds a gold-plated basket from Benin that Christina has had for thirty years, a Tahitian pearl, a piece of pre-Columbian jade, and a fabric pouch containing a sunflower seed from Ai Weiwei's show at Tate Modern.

02 Curtains That Glow

Twice a year, when Dosa's new fashion and housewares lines are unveiled, the loft is entirely reimagined: furniture gets cut down in size or painted and moved around, piles of soft rugs appear, and new curtains go up. Shown here are panels of handwoven handkerchief cotton with a border of Joshua trees silk-screened in a glow-in-the-dark fabric paint. The tree design was commissioned from Joshua Tree artists Deanna Thompson and Jeff Colson and used on Dosa dresses and a shawl; the curtains, however, are one-of-a-kind.

Rescued Office Fittings, LA Style

The dining area's tall cupboards are made from 1940s mahogany office doors that Lindon, who served as both architect and head builder, rescued from Dumpsters in the area. A friend of Christina's collected the bell jars for her from Paris flea markets; they display, among other things, branch coral, a Dansk candelabra, and an Indian falconer's stand. More local scrap lumber was used to make the dining table (see page 74).

Finding the Right Sink
All of the kitchen appliances, as well as the CECO double sink, were purchased used or as factory seconds on Craigslist. Lindon and Christina opted for an undermount sink so they could tile around it. The walls, counters, and shelves are all covered, hospital-style, in matte subway tiles.

03

04

03-05 A Kitchen with Nowhere to Hide

"Living in such an open space," says Christina, "really forces you to think about the choices you make. Most people have a lot of hiding spaces." Christina's attention extends to her dish soap (in a glass bottle with a bartender's spout) and sponge (found in a Oaxaca market). The kitchen's labware came from Columbia University's chemistry department via a New York flea market. She serves tea in vintage Heath Ceramics pottery with an olivewood spoon and a napkin from Kenya.

05

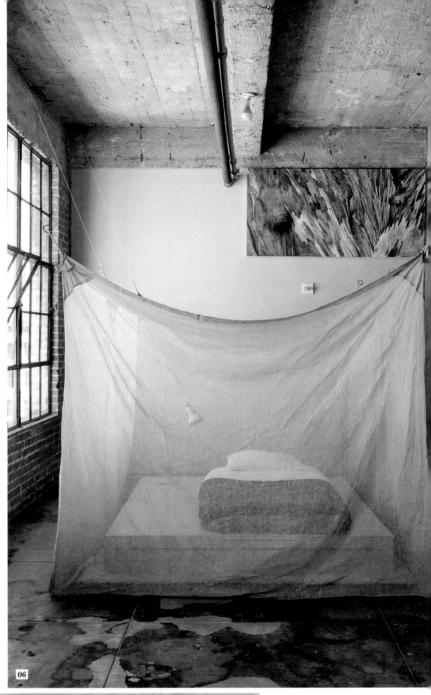

06 Camping Out at the Office

When Christina was in residence at 818 and flying insects became an issue, she cloaked a futon in a vintage Japanese mosquito net that had been hanging in the Dosa factory. The bed rests on a shearling rug and a gray-painted shipping crate. "I try not to bring in any new furniture," says Christina. "We just reuse and recycle." The paintings on the upper walls are by Judith Belzer.

07 Well Tucked, Dosa-Style

Christina applies dressmaker details to even the simplest bed. The indigo cover is a Dosa design, hand-spun, hand-loomed, and hand-dyed in India. The sheets are made from Libeco Home Belgian linen yardage that she edged in vintage Spanish lace.

The World's Best Guest Bed

When a friend of Christina's left Los Angeles for a job in New York, she parked her intricately carved Vietnamese opium bed in the loft. In addition to showcasing bedding designs, it often gets slept in. The open-door policy works thanks to organization: overnight guests at 818 are given a duffel bag with a comforter, sheets, towels, and instructions for how to wash the linens (in a machine in the kitchen) so they're ready for the next guest.

A Customized Public Bathroom
The kitchen's subway tiles reappear in the bathroom, which, at first glance, may look fairly standard. It's not. The steel towel bars were made for the space. And the exalted lighting (see opposite) sets off Dosa's bath designs: a Filikili rug made by women in the Konya area of Turkey using centuries-old techniques, and an orange handwoven cotton towel modeled after the ones Sadhus, professional religious men in India, wear around their shoulders.

08 A Rosy Light (from Hardware-Store Parts)

To introduce some warmth to a big space and create a bridge between the tiles and the concrete ceiling, Christina had Lindon create a Dan Flavin–like fluorescent ceiling light in a pale shade that verges on salmon.

09 The Hands-On Architect

Lindon built the recessed medicine cabinet using special hinges that allow the heavy mirror to hang flush with the wall. The glass-paneled door is another of his reclaimed 1940s office strays. Note that bare bulbs crop up throughout the loft, all of them easy on the eyes thanks to white tips, a subtle alternative to popular chrome tips, available from specialty lighting sources and Amazon.com.

Steal This Look

01
Minimalist Benches

In advance of an art opening and talk at 818, Lindon was recruited to come up with some easy seating. His solution: Donald Judd–like benches of salvaged Douglas fir (from floor joists and roof rafters) configured in two rectangular styles (see page 62). To make them: Plane the pieces flat (or use new wood) and trim to the size desired with a saw, then sand. Using an electric biscuit joiner, cut simple slots into the wood at the ends. Connect the seat and legs planks with glue and biscuits—flat, oval-shaped pieces of wood that are "like dowels," says Lindon, "but much easier to align." (The Woodworker's Guild of America offers short instructional videos on YouTube that explain how to use a biscuit joiner.) No finish is required. And, in addition to seating, the pieces work well as low display shelves.

02
Recycled Wood Table with Found Legs

Salvaged lumber was used to create a dining table top with a richly varied patina. The individual planks were planed and trimmed, and then glued and biscuited together—a job for a skilled woodworker. But the legs, seen above, were simply taken from a discarded folding table; they lend a beer-garden look.

03
Found Art

Edison bulbs used to illuminate Dosa 818 for a *Vanity Fair* Academy Awards dinner later found their way into a kitchen bowl. Like Marcel Duchamp readymades, they serve as a reminder that there can be poetry in the everyday.

04
Scrap Shower Shelf

A plank of Swiss pear—a prized wood often used for musical instruments and furniture because it doesn't warp—works well as a rustic shower ledge. Reports Lindon, "One of Christina's employees gave it to us. Every so often we add a few coats of oil, which makes it water resistant."

05
Homemade Cutting Boards

The tiniest fabric remnants get put to use at Dosa (see the appliquéd fabric hanging in Tiina Laakkonen's window, page 45). The Dosa way with leftover wood? Plane and sand it to form live-edge cutting boards.

Living in Black and White

Architectural designer Elizabeth Roberts's town house is packed with insider tricks for creating a clean look *and* staying on budget.

ABOVE: Elizabeth in her living room.

OPPOSITE: The black-and-white palette begins in the entry, which has its original marble floor. "The tiles aren't in great condition," says Elizabeth, "but I don't think it needs to be a perfect room—it's where you leave your shoes." She added a compact radiator from Governale, a Brooklyn company, which makes the space cozy and helps dry wet coats, boots, and umbrellas. The second set of doors is a smart original feature: it keeps the cold from rushing into the house.

Have you ever noticed how much more elegant the world looks when it's reduced to black and white? Designer Elizabeth Roberts has. Her Brooklyn home is a lesson in the benefits of hewing to a simple palette, resuscitating original details, and taking a no-tolerance approach to clutter. True, we can't all be quite so disciplined. But we can learn from the cost-conscious choices Elizabeth made when she set out to turn a warren of small, dark rooms into streamlined living quarters for her family of three (she's married to a doctor and they have a young son and a live-in au pair), plus a top-floor office big enough for her firm of five, Ensemble Architecture D.P.C.

"The building had been converted into an SRO with six tiny kitchens," says Elizabeth. "It was in terrible shape, which is how we were able to afford it." Working with a tight bottom line and a surprising number of Ikea and other off-the-shelf components, she gutted and retailored the 1866 Italianate structure. Having remodeled a number of historic town houses for clients, Elizabeth knew the dramatic benefits of opening up the main floor (which involved trussing the structure with a hidden network of steel). It's now bright and open with a living room big enough for a George sectional from B & B Italia, the furniture equivalent of a one-dish meal. An investment-piece sofa aside, she furnished the rooms sparingly and economically. The Viking stove, along with the kitchen's Carrara wall tiles, was found on Craigslist—you may think professionals get their best deals by using their to-the-trade discount with suppliers, but Elizabeth says the real bargains come thanks to the same dogged online research anyone can do.

We admire her practicality, her light-handed touch, and her high/low mix of materials. Elizabeth's stripped-down aesthetic gives resonance to every object and texture, enabling historic elements such as marble mantels and wood floors to speak with a soft but clear twenty-first-century accent.

Spruced-Up Stair

Elizabeth's son, Dean, shows off the winding backbone of the house. Because the steps need to be hard-wearing, they've been painted with high-gloss black floor paint—an affordable way to get a dramatic new look—and carpeted with a wool runner. "People always ask where I found the runner," says Elizabeth. "It's just wall-to-wall carpet that the installer trimmed and edged." As for the balusters, handrail, and floor, Elizabeth elected to have them dyed rather than stained.

The First Floor, Unveiled
By removing the supporting wall between the front parlor and the front hall, Elizabeth gave the 20-foot-wide first floor an extreme face-lift.

Good-Bye, Upper Cabinets

"Wall cabinets make a kitchen feel very kitchen-y," notes Elizabeth—which is precisely why she avoided them. Because the space is visible from the dining room, she wanted it to have the crispness of a white button-down shirt. Walls clad with honed Carrara marble tiles are offset by a shelf and counter of cast concrete, an intentional mix of the formal and the rugged. The cabinets and knobs are from Ikea.

01 Fireplace Makeover

In the dining room, Elizabeth raised the existing firebox to eye level and inserted a Tuscan Italian Grill from Bella Cucina—a basic, inexpensive metal grate that stands over kindling and enables the family to barbecue and grill pizzas indoors.

02 The Pros and Cons of Bench Seating

Elizabeth picked the waxed-oak Big Sur table—a Crate & Barrel basic—for its minimalist lines and ability to take a beating. Her choice of benches instead of chairs offers distinct benefits and drawbacks: they hold as many as five people on each side, and kids love to lie on them, but Elizabeth warns that "you have to coordinate scooting in with your neighbors, and you get pretty chummy with the person next to you."

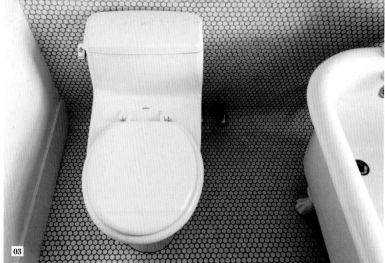

03

04

03-04 Penny Tiles Everywhere

In the guest bathroom, Elizabeth inventively applied inexpensive 1-inch-by-1-inch penny round tiles from Daltile not just on the floor but running up the wall, creating an uninterrupted pattern and eliminating potentially grimy corners. Elizabeth always specifies matte tiles for bathrooms because the surface is less slippery than that of glossy tiles. Gray grout is another of her essentials for a tile floor: "White grout in a trafficked space quickly turns gray and looks dirty and uneven."

05 Black and White for All Sizes

A bare wood floor in Dean's room is perfect for Legos. The bed is one of Ikea's most popular designs, and the world map above it, a framed classroom model from the sixties, was purchased on eBay for $100. Vintage drawers are topped with a French poster; it drives home Elizabeth's palette and looks perfectly finished in an Ikea ready-made frame.

NOUS SOMMES ENSEMBLE.

06 Bedroom Basics

The original marble mantel with a French wall sticker (from thecollection.fr) and a Roberts radio is all the visual excitement the master bedroom needs. The bed, a standard Ikea design, is simply a box spring with legs. The Missoni wool throw was a wedding present.

Bathroom Savings and Splurges

The master bath seamlessly mixes high and low elements. For the floors, Elizabeth used 1-inch-by-2-inch statuary honed Thassos marble tiles (available from Thassos.com) with gray grout. She cut costs by lining the walls with affordable subway tiles (with white grout) from Daltile. Her pedestal sink, a Marc Newson design, has since been discontinued, but it's much like Duravit's Happy D Washbasin, a high-end choice balanced by Elizabeth's use of a Speakman faucet and showerhead: "They're made for hotels and institutions, so they're workhorses. And they look and feel good."

08

07   Bedroom Up Yonder

On the town house's top floor, where Elizabeth's office is located, she introduced an in-law studio. A black ladder from New York's Putnam Rolling Ladder Co. leads to the room's loft bed tucked under an existing skylight. It previously provided natural light to the bathroom below and is now for "moon gazing." (A blackout blind for it is on the to-do list.)

08   A Capsule Apartment

The space is used not only for guests but also as a conference room and occasional classroom for Dean's roving preschool group. The kitchen is composed of Ikea Applåd cabinets kitted out with a dorm-size fridge, a stainless counter from a restaurant supply store on the Bowery, and a GE stovetop from Sears. Custom overhead shelves hold a Kenmore combination convection oven and microwave—"You can actually bake in it," notes Elizabeth, "so it's a complete mini kitchen."

Steal This Look

01
Cast Concrete Counters

Concrete isn't an inexpensive material for a shelf or counter—it costs about the same as Corian or Carrara marble. "Its advantages are that it's seamless and can be cast in any shape you want," says Elizabeth. "The flip side is it chips and stains easily." Elizabeth used it for the first time in her own kitchen and reports, "I like its simplicity and honesty; the negatives are there, but they don't bother me."

02
Carrara Marble Tiles in the Kitchen

Marble slabs are expensive, but marble cut pieces don't have to be—after all, they're often made from leftovers. And they're especially well priced if you go for variations that aren't pure white. Elizabeth bought her 3-inch-by-6-inch matte tiles from a New Jersey wholesaler who was unloading remnants on Craigslist.

03
Dyed Wood Floors

Because the floors in the house were a combination of new and old wood, which absorb stains differently, Elizabeth opted to dye all of her oak parquet floors a rich brown that verges on black. "Dye is like rubbing Sharpie ink all over the wood. It absorbs completely and evenly." She used Woodsong, a product by M. L. Campbell, and mixed dark mocha and black in equal proportions. Warning—it's a very messy process. If possible, get a professional to do it for you.

04
Unorthodox Upholstery

Traditional upholstery fabric is often expensive. Elizabeth makes use of hard-wearing—and affordable—alternatives: men's suit wool and, shown here, African mudcloth from YaraAfricanFabrics.com, a shop on 125th Street in Harlem.

05
Living Room Turned Screening Room

Whenever possible, Elizabeth adds a projector across from an expanse of wall, as she did in her living room opposite the mantel. It cost about $800, plus another $500 to install it while the walls and ceilings were open (digital versions keep coming out that are smaller and less expensive). Turn off the lights, flick on a movie or the television, and you have your own home theater.

Personality, Not Perfection

Others would have found Justine Hand's old Cape Cod cottage in dire need of updating. But she saw that all it required was someone who understood it. To Justine, "the ubiquitous impulse for perfection is soulless."

ABOVE: Justine and her family packing up for the beach. They first got to know their 1807 house by renting it for summer vacations.

OPPOSITE: Justine paired the guest room's original wallpaper with Ikea curtains and an iron bed frame bought on eBay—"So graceful," she notes, "it looks like a spider wove it."

Justine Hand has an affinity for the secondhand, the homemade, and the humble, gravitating to everyday objects with stories to tell (though she prefers that they speak in a whisper). Light glancing across an outdoor clothesline, a cup of tea made from her own mint, kids playing on a hammock, pokeberry weeds in a Vaseline glass vase: these are Justine's moments. Not coincidentally, she spends her days writing about such things for her blog DesignSkool as well as for Remodelista. The daughter of an astrologer (with a PhD in medieval studies) and a wildlife conservationist, she has her mind in the stars and her feet on the ground.

Justine and her family—her husband, Chad, and their two young children, Oliver and Solvi—live outside of Boston, and for many summers they rented a rose-covered cottage on Rock Harbor in Cape Cod, immediately across from Justine's grandparents' house (and not far from the house where Justine grew up). When the owner of the cottage was ready to sell, he set out to find not the highest bidder, but the person he felt would do the old place justice. It can't have been much of a contest: no one could love its egg-yolk-yellow kitchen, spatter-painted floors, and wonky, two-toned screen doors as much as Justine.

But that's not to say that Salt Timber Cottage, as the house is known, hasn't required work. Dating to 1807 and last overhauled in the 1940s, it suffered from a common case of New England dowdiness. Relying on little more than paint, the singular Cape Cod light, and a careful selection of secondhand furnishings and accessories, Justine recast the rooms in her own light. Her mantra: "Personality, not perfection."

01 A Swedish Palette

The favorite hangout at Salt Timber Cottage, the porch is painted Benjamin Moore Linen White offset by a floor in Benjamin Moore Stonington Gray—an intentionally Gustavian combination that Justine carried over into several rooms to tie the house together. She painted the ceiling in Martin-Senour Paints Chinastone, a yellow that looks as if it meandered in from the kitchen.

02 Signifiers of Summer

Washing dishes at the cottage is an enticement for Justine because the sink overlooks the family clothesline and hammock. "In the summer," she commented on her blog, "actually taking the time to 'perform' tasks like cleaning up is almost a Zen exercise."

Making Room for Error

The dining room is the heart of the cottage, and a fine example of Justine's perfectly imperfect design aesthetic. She had the custom-built drop-leaf table modeled after a smaller Pierre Deux design with a raw-wood top—she wanted something that would "get marked and show wine rings." It's made of old pine that Justine's aunt Sheila, an architect (see page 109), whitewashed by applying thinned paint and rubbing it off with a rag. The chairs are mismatched but unified by three coats of the same Benjamin Moore Linen White used on the doors and trim. The walls are in Tidewater from Martin-Senour Paints.

03-04 Heirlooms Not Required

"Our cottage," Justine writes, "is a bit of sanctuary from the real world." On the dining table, lavender and veronica surrounded by mercury glass votives form a simple centerpiece. And in a corner of the room, a cloudy mirror in a gilded frame is paired with a well-worn gilded chair. Like so many details in the house, they look as if they've always been there. In fact, they're all Justine's foraged finds, introduced like props to portray a compelling domestic scene.

05 An Edited Take on the Pantry

Conveniently located off the dining room, the pantry offers a simple lesson in curating a collection. Rather than use the shelves as catchalls, Justine displays a carefully chosen lineup of useful things, including the hand-shaped bisque vases and Wedgwood pot she selected from her grandmother's packed china cabinet. On their own, they're much more interesting and meaningful than if lost in a hodgepodge.

06   Going with the Gold

The sunny kitchen with a peaked ceiling and black beams was preserved as is, including its icebox (now used for storage) and half picnic table (see page 106). Justine simply touched up the paint and accessorized well. "Yellow," she says, "is so hard to get right. I might not have been so daring if this hadn't been here, but I'm glad it was."

07   An Old Kitchen Full of Fresh Ideas

Among the room's smart touches, the windows make use of limited wall space by sliding sideways (rather than up and down), and a wooden screen door has an ingenious band of black painted across the middle, exactly where fingerprints congregate, to keep it looking pristine.

08   Cape Light Enhanced

One of the most appealing features of the kitchen is that it has windows on three sides. To supplement the sun, Justine added a vintage pendant light with a milk glass shade found at Solstice Home, one of her go-to sources on Etsy. No wiring needed: thanks to a presentable cloth cord (shown opposite, and available from SundialWire.com), it's casually rigged with an extension cord.

09-10 The Reinvented Shed

Justine resourcefully turned an unused gardener's hut into what Oliver and Solvi call the Three Bears House. In addition to whitewashing the interior, she painted the child-sized furniture and decorated with bird's nests. Now, when Justine tells her kids to play in the yard, they have the perfect place to go.

Peak Sleeping Conditions

The master bedroom is tucked under the eaves on the second floor. Though just big enough for a double bed, it feels open and airy thanks to the powers of Justine's Swedish palette: the floor is Benjamin Moore Stonington Gray, and all the other elements of the room, aside from a bouquet of nasturtiums, are in restful shades of earth and sky.

11 Cape Cod Clinical

The 1940s bathrooms, one upstairs, one down, take their look from hospital design: "No architectural flourishes," says Justine, "just great light on a human scale." She furnished this one with an old enamelware wastebasket on wheels and a metal cabinet that might have come out of a doctor's office but in fact is from Pottery Barn.

Steal This Look

01

Foraged Bouquets

When she arrives at the cottage, Justine has a one-two routine: after putting perishables in the fridge, she immediately heads out to the garden with snippers in hand to freshen every room with wildflowers. When nothing is in bloom, branches, leaves, and grasses do the trick: "People forget that green is a color," she says. For vases, she uses everything from milk bottles to cordial glasses.

02

The Half Picnic Table

Many years ago, someone had the inspired idea of trimming a picnic table to fit in a corner of the kitchen. Painted the same egg-yolk yellow as the walls and icebox, it serves as a work surface and counter.

04
The Organized Bathroom Shelf

In lieu of a medicine cabinet, the upstairs bath features inset shelves with contents on full view. To avoid a tangle of toiletries and tools, Justine corrals the pieces in small containers made of natural materials: see-through baskets, a juice glass, a flowerpot, whatever she has on hand. The results: not only ordered but interesting, a combination worth replicating in any display.

03
The Minimalist Mantel

Justine advocates stripping mantels down to a few interesting objects—here, a circular wood frame and a bleached antler. "I used to try to layer things the way stylists do, but last year, when I repainted, I had to remove it all and I didn't put it back."

05
Well-Placed Outlets

Rather than set into baseboards, where they clutter sight lines, the cottage's original electrical outlets are discreetly positioned on the floor in all the right spots for lamps. For how to re-create an old spattered floor like this one, see page 273.

Streamlined Yankee

Cape Cod architect Sheila Narusawa poured a career's worth of smart solutions into her idyll by the sea. And behind closed doors, she sets new standards for household organization.

ABOVE: Sheila not only designed her house but takes a daily hands-on approach to its upkeep.

OPPOSITE: The house is situated on the property's highest elevation, a south-facing ridge that overlooks the water. Made to withstand salt air and dramatic seasons, the detailing is a sophisticated take on Cape Cod classics: white clapboard siding, an angled cedar-shingled roof, and breezy porches.

Her prospective client had in mind a tower, something vaguely nautical that would take advantage of the views on offer on an untouched peninsula overlooking the Atlantic. Sheila Narusawa found the approach a tad predictable and started thinking of ways to "not make a tower a cliché." She no doubt had other things on her mind, too: Moncrieff Cochran, or "Mon," the inheritor of this piece of extraordinary real estate, had been her eighth-grade boyfriend, and they were reconnecting for the first time in years. Both had grown up right here, in the town of Orleans on Cape Cod. And both had left the area and eventually returned. Mon, a child psychologist, was divorced with two grown kids. Sheila, also divorced, had practiced architecture in Tokyo, and later in Boston, before resettling close to her two sisters and father. Mon signed Sheila on for the job, and somewhere along the way she found herself designing a house for the two of them.

Sheila's style is a combination of New England practicality and Japanese craftsmanship, shot through with a Scandinavian love of light. The couple's white clapboard house—completed in 2009, shortly after their wedding—is both modest in scale (1,800 square feet) and a complex kit of parts. It takes inspiration from the best of the local building vocabulary, but in an abstract way. Its many vantages call to mind, among other things, a one-room schoolhouse, an open-winged seagull, a ship's bow, and the sloping folds of an origami crane. It's a secluded place tailor-built for two. To maximize sun and air, the structure is a single room wide, with windows on three sides, creating a current of cross breezes that makes air-conditioning and even ceiling fans unnecessary. A backyard wind turbine—the area's first—supplies all of the electricity. And Mon got his wish for a tower: a second-story lookout is devoted to the master suite—and to views that allow the couple (who eschew window coverings) to fall asleep in moonlight and wake up with the sun.

01 Creation Story

Perched on a bookshelf, the original architectural model serves as a happy reminder of how the house—and the couple's new life together—began.

02 Decorations Courtesy of Mother Nature

Like so many designers, Sheila loves the visual drama that comes from mixing materials. In the living room she lined shelves with books, art, driftwood, and a layered display of razor clam shells gathered on nearby beaches. Together the shells create an arresting textured pattern.

03 The Central Corridor

Each of the rooms cants off the center at a different angle, creating a dynamism inside and out. Here, the downstairs hall, bright with windows and glass-paneled doors, veers from kitchen to office to living room.

The Light and Bright Approach

The kitchen's updated Carl Larsson appeal comes from the fact that there's so much visible pale wood, starting at the ceiling, which is poplar sealed with PPG Seal Grip acrylic primer. The cabinets are made of shiplapped poplar, an old Cape tongue-and-groove construction. The floor, an inexpensive Eastern white pine, was ragged with a custom-mixed Benjamin Moore shade of warm gray flat latex (see page 120 for more on Sheila's floor treatments). They're not just pretty—thanks to a subfloor of radiant heat, the floors warm the whole house even in the height of winter.

Proportions Perfected

Sheila and Mon's dining table (also pictured on pages 112 and 120), a wedding gift from his siblings, was made by a brother-in-law. Inspired by an antique trestle table that Sheila coveted, it was built to her exacting specs. It's 8 feet long and 30 inches wide, the "magic numbers if you want a design that has room for people and tableware, but still allows for intimate conversations." Similarly, the windows are scaled just right. Made by Andersen, they're 65 inches high with sills lowered to only 19 inches above the floor. Explains Sheila, "The size and lowered sills extend the feeling of bringing the outside in and introduce a groundedness. I used muntined windows vs. plate glass because I wanted a slight barrier; with plate glass the whole space seems to leak out."

04

04 The Liberated Kitchen

To avoid encumbering the room with kitchen things, Sheila consolidated all of the storage. A bank of tall, whitewashed wood cabinets with pullout shelves contains not only pantry goods but also the microwave and toaster, plugged in and ready to use (see page 287). The fridge, too, is camouflaged behind these doors. And on the opposite side of the kitchen, there's under-the-counter storage and windows with ocean views. The overall results are sensible and understated.

05-06 A System for Everything

There's a satisfying order to the kitchen, down to the mug lineup and, at the opposite end of the counter, the ladles, measuring cups, and other essentials that hang on steel bars from German manufacturer Rösle.

05

06

07

07 Old Wood, New Sink

To inject texture and warmth into the upstairs bathroom, Sheila set the sink into a counter of barn siding. She left the under plumbing exposed and was careful to select a model with stainless fittings rather than PVC ones.

08 Indoor-Outdoor Bath

A bright yellow paneled door leads to the downstairs bath, positioned so that those just in from the beach can rinse off in an outdoor shower, hang their suits on pegs, and come in for a soak. The claw-foot tub is made by Sunrise Specialty. Charm aside, its selling point is its length: at 5 feet 6 inches, it's big enough for two.

08

The Combination Office–Guest Loft

Sheila's office has 11-foot ceilings and, in keeping with her waste-not-want-not approach, does double duty as runover sleeping quarters thanks to a loft (which contains a pair of twin mattresses accessed via a rolling ladder). The stainless-steel railing and steel wire cables were fabricated at nearby Nauset Marina and are exactly what's used on ships.

09

10

09 The Room with the Views

A small second-story aerie forms the master suite, a peak-roofed meditative space where everything has its place. The custom platform bed contains deep drawers for blankets, suitcases, and runover from the adjoining dressing room (picture impeccably folded sweaters topped with Japanese red silk sachets). Sheila line-dries the bedsheets, even in winter—"They smell so good"—and, like most architects, prefers an extremely tucked-in look.

10 A Place to Perch

The spareness of the room allows for uninterrupted views, not only of the surrounding landscape—the balcony overlooks the Atlantic—but also of a prized antique Windsor bench, inspiring a visitor to comment that the space could be used for a Quaker meeting. A family heirloom, the bench was a wedding present from Mon's mother.

11   Controlled Color

Against a palette of warm whites, grays, and blacks, only punctuation points of color crop up—a vase of nasturtiums here, a bright yellow door there—and very little in the way of pattern. This level of design policing is what gives the house its combination of rigor and serenity.

12   Mirror as Mood Enhancer

To keep the master bath from feeling chilly, Sheila hung an atmospheric, slightly foxed mirror on a pristine white wall. Beneath it a shelf of perfume bottles and his-and-hers striped Japanese towels add visual interest and underscore the sense of order.

Steal This Look

01
Pale Wood Floors

For Sheila, figuring out how to achieve matte floors that don't yellow over time is an ongoing obsession, one that she traces to her Norwegian roots. Throughout the house, she ragged the white pine floors a pale gray—a process that involves applying paint by hand with a moist sponge and rubbing it off with a rag. She finished it with Danish company Woca's Woca Soap, but in high-traffic areas, such as the kitchen, the results erode, so she's considering succumbing to a coat of matte polyurethane. And next time, she wants to try Woca's liquid lye, which permanently lightens soft woods. Needless to say, shoes are not welcome inside.

02
A Sunny Door

Sheila's doors, it will come as no surprise, are custom-made using 1¾-inch-thick mahogany planks and tongue-and-groove construction inside and out. The yellow, however, is straight-from-the-can Benjamin Moore Luminous Day from its MoorGlo soft gloss acrylic line.

03
Lampshade Wall Light

In the guest room, the back side of a bookshelf serves as a tall headboard. Sheila created its built-in sconces using nothing more than a pair of hardware-store sockets, incandescent bulbs, and linen-covered clamp-on lamp shades.

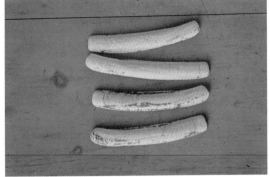

04
Stacked Shell Display

Razor clam shells are plentiful on Cape Cod's ocean beaches (and so named because they look like old-fashioned straight razors). Sheila finds them washed ashore often covered in dried seaweed. Before each makes it onto her shelf, she scrubs it with pumice found on the beach and leaves it outside to bleach in the sun.

05
The Under $500 Powder Room

Sheila tucked a trim guest bath with a sliding door into the front hall, and decided to keep it as inexpensive as possible while sticking with pieces she genuinely likes. With rough plumbing already in place, the costs (not including labor) were as follows: Sterling toilet, $140; Gerber West Point Space Saver sink, $61; Gerber faucet, $82; and wood towel hook, $25. And that, along with an Ikea print, a pitcher of dried berries, and a basket of toilet paper, is all the room needs.

06
Chair as Bedside Table

In the guest room, a Gothic hall chair is put to work as a bedside table (one that's positioned at the foot of the bed because space is tight). Against a simple backdrop, it looks sculptural but not overly serious—especially with a bentwood Chinese lamp perched on it like an exotic bird.

The New Romantics

In Michelle McKenna and Brenlen Jinkens's restored 1840s London town house, powdery paints, chinoiserie wallpaper, and the occasional ceramic butterfly point the way to a fanciful detour in decorating. We predict it's the look of the future.

ABOVE: The family romping in their yard, which they enclosed with reclaimed London bricks.

OPPOSITE: In the dining room, a Swedish table from Stolab.se is paired with Victorian spoon-back chairs upholstered in a "not very practical" white-on-cream Marimekko brocade that Brenlen brought back from a business trip to Sweden. "I like juxtapositions," says Michelle. "Marimekko is contemporary; brocade is unexpected."

See Michelle and Brenlen's powder room on pages 242–245.

When Michelle McKenna and Brenlen Jinkens placed the winning bid on a Georgian town house in London's Clerkenwell neighborhood, it was in such a derelict state that it was essentially a blank canvas. The required renovation could have taken it back to its handsome original 1840s state, with late-Edwardian fittings. Or the house could have been gutted and gone clean and contemporary. For Michelle, who guided the work and orchestrated the interiors, the answer was clear: she blazed her own trail.

Unorthodox living quarters are nothing new to the couple. Before their move, they had been quite at home living with their two young boys in a basketball-court-sized loft with a seventy-step entrance. Brenlen is an investment banker, an accomplished cook, and "a real peacock," says Michelle. As for Michelle, she had a stellar international career in advertising before returning to school and becoming a practitioner of *amatsu*, a Japanese healing art. The Clerkenwell house was her first full-immersion design experience, but she says her work history prepared her well. ("Managing a budget and a group of creative people requires a very similar skill set.") So, too, did her innate color sense and willingness to heed her own instincts.

The 3,000-square-foot structure had long ago fallen on hard times; extreme water damage and a crowd of marginal occupants had taken their toll. "Walking on the stairs was life-threatening," says Michelle. She worked with a friend, architect Rahesh Ram of Naau Architecture, to painstakingly return the building to a single-family house. Getting there involved, among other things, rebuilding the spiraling five-story stair, restoring the latch-and-plaster walls (and painting them with luminous and permeable distemper paints), refurbishing windows, and excavating ceiling roses with a wire brush. But it wasn't until Michelle began adding her own imprint that things got especially interesting. No one can say what exactly inspired her to introduce chinoiserie wallpaper to a classic English kitchen. Or to go to town with buttercream pastels and a sprinkling of grandmotherly tchotchkes. The results, in the words of Michelle's feng shui adviser, are "very yang." Translation: they're a new, feminine version of the British eccentric look.

One-Third of the House Is Stairs

The building has only two rooms per floor, and a lot of stairs. Rescuing the staircase, one of the only original features in the house, required a structural engineer, metal supports, and all new spindles. This view provides a glimpse of a Victorian ceiling rose mounted on the wall and the downstairs powder room with neo-Victorian wallpaper from Timorous Beasties.

A Velvet Revolution

Michelle reupholstered a stately Chesterfield in a blue-green silk velvet from Mulberry that works well against the moody white-gray walls, which took several tries to get right (they're a 50/50 mix of Farrow & Ball's Cornforth White and Strong White). In need of a place to store firewood, Michelle got her contractor to insert a shelf in a recessed wall. "It looks decorative, but it's utterly functional." As for the Georges Braque over the mantel, it's an affordable print in an antique frame.

01 A Pinch of This and That

At one end of the kitchen, a surprising mix of ingredients—Swedish chairs, a built-in green leather banquette, a Louis Poulsen copper Artichoke light, and chinoiserie wallpaper—work well together thanks to a harmonious palette.

02 An International Menu

"We're always here, so shouldn't it be the nicest room in the house?" asks Michelle, by way of explaining the thinking behind the kitchen. Throughout the house, she worked closely with furniture-making brothers Ben and Tim Goodingham. The Goodinghams designed and constructed the cabinets, cooktop island, and cherry counters, taking inspiration from British firm Plain English's distilled versions of the classics. The brass handles came out of a Lake District hotel via Michelle's "salvage guy," Edward Haes (haes.co.uk). As for the chinoiserie wallpaper, Michelle first spotted it on a greeting card and traced it to British company Fromental. It gives the room a roguish dash of formality—and remains, she reports, miraculously free of food splashes.

03-04 Two Sinks, One Mirror, and the Prettiest Pink Chair

Arguably the most charming room in the house, the vast master bath has twin pedestal sinks (with nonmatching nickel faucets from Horus) and an oval Italian mirror found at Retrouvius. The trash can is an antique that Michelle wishes someone would reproduce. The resting spot is a nineteenth-century nursing chair reupholstered in Designer's Guild linen.

Chinoiserie, Upstairs and Down

Like the kitchen, the master bath presents a successful mash-up of modernism, British traditionalism, and chinoiserie. Fully open to the room, the glass-walled shower is lined with a tile mural from Fired Earth and has a slate floor flanked by slatted teak.

05 Tall Tub

By buying salvaged fixtures—some old, some of recent vintage—Michelle and Brenlen got the old-fashioned designs they wanted and saved money. The extralong enameled bath came with nickel faucets. To give it a dressy prominence, the exterior of the tub is painted in Raw Earth, a taupe from Fired Earth's Kevin McCloud collection, with feet in a blend of silver and gold.

06 A Touch of Magic

Every element in the room holds its own, down to the dark-edged enamelware soap dish that pops out against white porcelain.

07 White on White or Gray

Michelle and Brenlen are believers in the bedroom as sanctuary: minimal art, no closets, and stools as tables. Michelle bought the headboard from Shoreditch antiques shop Maison Trois Garçons and upholstered it in a soothing purple-gray velvet.

08 Rose-Scented Sleep

The exception to the empty bedroom approach: plants and homemade bouquets are welcome. But sparingly. Quiet is still the rule.

Dream-Inducing Wallpaper and Lights

Michelle and Brenlen's boys, Aidan and Tiernan, eight and nine, slumber under fanciful Josef Frank wallpaper from Svenskt Tenn in Stockholm and 1960s balloon-shaped wall lights by Luxus, Vittsjö. (Michelle found them in their original boxes at Stockholm's Domino Antik.)

Steal This Look

01
The Tactile Sofa

Textured materials are the visual equivalent of spices: they bring things alive. The living room sofa is layered with an unorthodox but harmonious trio: silk velvet, a vintage patterned cotton pillow, and a curly gray sheepskin from Gotland, Sweden.

02
Cupboard Built from an Old Door

You don't always have to shell out for antiques when you're after a vintage look. In need of a sink-side bathroom cabinet, Michelle had her crew build one using an old door. The piece was inspired by, and serves as a companion piece to, the room's French marriage cupboard (shown on page 131).

03
Fringed Trim

Michelle's daring addition of pink and yellow tasseled ribbon on the edge of her Marimekko upholstered seats is an easy look to pull off. She had an upholsterer do it, but all it takes is a glue gun. Good-looking fringe is hard to come by: it's available online from London shop VV Rouleaux (vvrouleaux.com).

04
Retro Phone Table

One of the most notable details in the kitchen is a wall shelf bearing a pink phone: a reproduction Princess (with push buttons) purchased on Amazon.com for about $33. The color choices—shell pink against walls painted in Farrow & Ball's Pale Powder, and a green banquette—are what make the arrangement memorable.

05
Pastel Shades

White may be the default color for window covers, but it's worth considering an unexpected alternative: palest pink. An extremely flattering shade, it counters gloomy skies and telegraphs happiness.

The Anglophiles' Retreat

Leaving the trappings of the twenty-first century far behind, book designer Megan Wilson and painter Duncan Hannah invented their own otherworldly book-filled getaway.

ABOVE: The couple in country mode. (Megan is wearing men's WW I army trousers bought on eBay.)

OPPOSITE: The star attraction of the dining room is a giant, canvas-backed, foldable driving map of England discovered in a bookstore on the King's Road in London for £5. The green-glass pendant light from Rejuvenation is Megan's salute to the Churchill War Rooms.

By day, Megan Wilson creates artful book covers as the design director of Knopf's Vintage Books. Her portfolio covers the canon of Western greats, from *Dracula* to *Lolita* and all of the Jane Austens. By night, she runs our favorite online store, Ancient Industries, a collection of British and European goods that focuses on the tried and true: objects, as she puts it, of "humble purpose, elegant form." Among the offerings are enamelware porridge pots, merino hunting socks, tartan throws, and ticking oven mitts, all made the same way for decades, even centuries. (She's so expert on the world's best everyday objects that we recruited her to write "The Remodelista 100," which starts on page 295.)

Megan grew up in Weston, Connecticut, until age seven, when her family decamped for London, where she went on to study graphic design at Saint Martins School of Art. She and her husband, fellow Anglophile Duncan Hannah, a painter whose work is in the collection of the Metropolitan Museum of Art, live in a small New York apartment and an 1830s four-bedroom house in Cornwall, Connecticut. The Cornwall place is an ongoing project that they purchased pretty much sight unseen. "I thought, how bad could it be?" says Megan, "and then I saw how bad. I wanted to sell it immediately."

"There had been a fire in the 1970s," explains Duncan. "It was as gloomy and suburban as you can get."

Operating on a tight budget, they've reinvented every inch of it themselves, thanks mainly to what Megan calls "the miracle of paint and stripped carpet." Miracle is right. The two now live a bucolic life amid tall hedges, steep stairs, books galore, and Duncan's carefully curated collections: toy cars, model ships, vintage movie star photos, and pencils in shades of red, to name a few. A laptop and an iPhone have been allowed in, but there are next to no other signs of the mass-made, the plastic, or the new. In lieu of Kleenex, there are handkerchiefs. Laundry soap is doled out of an enamelware bin. And reading is done in the library. But make no mistake: this is no museum. It's a way to live, according to two visionaries.

01

01 A Library Invented from Whole Cloth

Megan and Duncan transformed what they considered the gloomiest room—a dark, second-floor spare bedroom—into a library that looks as if it came with the house. The room holds some three thousand volumes of fiction organized alphabetically: "There are so many books, we had to do it," says Duncan.

02 Cover Girl

A Truman Capote cover designed by Megan, who specializes in resuscitating classics.

How to Exercise a Wall

Formerly home to, in Megan's words, "a pyromaniac ten-year-old who painted a mural of Satan on the wall," the guest room is now one of the nicest spots in the house. Its walls are the palest lilac, a color Duncan mixed to Megan's specs: "I wanted something between pink and violet, more red than lavender." A mix of prints and drawings is hung salon-style. Duncan laid out the framed arrangement on the floor before installing it. "It's like putting together a puzzle. When you hang work in a group, the art has a dialogue."

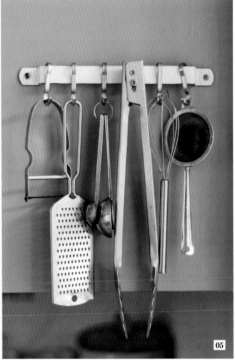

03 Accessories with a British Accent

The kitchen window is edged with nests perched in terra-cotta pots and Mochaware mugs. The bistro curtains—to let sun in but keep prying eyes out—are made from an Ian Mankin stripe called Odeon (Megan had her dry cleaner do the stitching).

04-05 A Kitchen Reinvented with Paint

Without doing any demolition, but making ample use of Farrow & Ball's Folly Green paint, Megan transformed a 1970s beige kitchen into a model of the English cottage style (helped along by classics like an enamelware bar, above, with hooks for hanging utensils). The Formica counters are painted with Benjamin Moore Fresh Start primer followed by Benjamin Moore Decorators White. The brown ceramic knobs are from Rejuvenation. The cosmetic improvements extend to the vinyl floor: Megan brushed it with a loose gray and white check using Benjamin Moore porch paint.

Lost Worlds Recaptured
The back half of the first floor is devoted to Duncan's studio. His paintings evoke glamorous lost eras. Duncan himself has described his art as clips from his boyhood imaginings (see his work at DuncanHannah.blogspot.com).

06 The Past Is Present

In the master bedroom, a steamer trunk is the perfect height to work as a bedside table. Much of what the couple lives with is either of their own creation or vintage (yes, that's a working candlestick telephone).

07 Fresco Courtesy of Zip-Strip

Not afraid to get dirty, Duncan used Zip-Strip and donned a gas mask to scrape the paint from a bedroom door before refinishing it. Along the way, he decided he liked the moody, fresco-like results. "It takes several sessions," he advises. "You're done whenever it looks good to you." He has the sense to know that some things are left well enough alone: the velvet chair is just as it arrived from a yard sale.

08 Power in Numbers

The powder room is lined with old group photos collected over the years at flea markets in London and New York. Their sepia tones work well against chocolate-brown walls and a green pedestal sink found at a tag sale on Route 7.

Steal This Look

02
Soap Decanter

In keeping with a no-plastics-in-the-house rule, dish soap is dispensed from a glass cruet intended for olive oil or vinegar (see "The Remodelista 100," page 297).

03
The Properly Detailed Front Door

A well-accessorized entry makes a big impact. After replacing a 1970s door with a nineteenth-century one, the couple set about styling it. The Victorian knocker came from eBay, and a trip to Au Petit Bonheur la Chance in Paris resulted in enameled numbers for here and all the other doors in the house.

01
The Low-Cost Art Gallery

Duncan likes displaying art salon-style, and his approach to framing is refreshingly low-budget: he keeps a stash of yard-sale frames—"I like the distress on them"—and puts them to use by pairing them with new mats cut by a framer. Mats, he specifies, are best in shades of off-white ("never pure white") and gray.

04
Penguins en Masse

We love the look of classic, well-thumbed Penguin paperbacks in red (travel and adventure), blue (biography), green (crime), and orange (fiction). They can be found at used-book stores and are still being published. Duncan paints trompe l'oeil facsimiles of the covers, including one titled *Cautionary Tales by Duncan Hannah,* while Megan sticks to the real thing, grouping them on shelves in the powder room. Displayed together, they pack a punch.

05
Trompe l'Oeil Runner

In a nod to the backstairs style of old English houses, Megan saved money by painting steps with "a poor man's runner." After applying two coats of Benjamin Moore's Linen White in semigloss and letting it dry, she taped off the runner (23 inches wide, with a 5-inch border on each side) and painted it with a Benjamin Moore oil-based porch paint. Because the stairs are old and crooked, getting the lines right required measuring each step, as well as standing back to eyeball the whole.

A Whiter Shade of Pale

Only creams and neutrals pass the threshold of designer Michaela Scherrer's exquisitely imagined quarters. Follow her approach for rooms that impart clarity and calm.

ABOVE: Michaela and menagerie in her home office.

OPPOSITE: With its polished concrete floor and pale walls, the dining room calls to mind a chapel. Built-in cupboards that read as recessed paneling allow the few furnishings and objects to take center stage. The steel and silk-cord light, an interpretation of a seventeenth-century chandelier, is by British firm Bowles and Linares. Cappellini's Fronzoni '64 metal chairs were chosen, Michaela admits, for their simplicity of line rather than for comfort (she remedied that by having leather cushions made for them).

In her thirty-six years as an interior designer, Michaela Scherrer has developed a prescriptive approach to color. "Every shade has a vibration that affects your body," she says, noting that red stresses nerves and should be avoided in the bedroom, while blue is calming and restful. According to Michaela, brown imparts a grounded feeling. And green, preferably introduced via plants, is a pick-me-up—one that she came to know intimately growing up in leafy Pasadena, California.

Nuanced colors make their way into Michaela's work for her clients, but rarely the bold or the bright (the petal-strewn spa bath in plaster and teak is one of her signatures). And in the corner of Pasadena where she currently lives with her two dogs and cat, she long ago cast her rooms in whites: "I spend my days looking at so many things, studying people in their spaces. I need tranquility at home."

Not surprisingly, Michaela is a devotee of meditation. The ascetic approach, however, is not exactly her style. Instead, she's all about aligning the mind, body, spirit—and sofa. Her 1,500-square-foot bungalow was built in the 1920s as a bird sanctuary for the estate next door. The last feathers were cleared out in the 1960s when the director of the Pasadena Playhouse converted it from Mediterranean roost to French Regency folly. Michaela erased his decorating but did very little in the way of construction. What she did do was paint and furnish, pile books, and make collages, all in her ethereal style. Cloaked in a rainbow of pales, the house has a fresh guise: it's easy to imagine it existing inside a cloud.

The Decluttering Power of White

Michaela's designs are meditative but not monastic. She's fascinated by the interplay of textures and tones and the way natural materials play off one another. Here, using simple shapes—boxes, small plaster vessels by artist Maggie Hazen, and books (page-side out to work with her light palette)—she created a tranquil shelf tableau. "Living with white doesn't take a lot of discipline," she insists. "If you have different colors and things are in disarray, it's obvious. If you have one color and things are in disarray, it just looks artistic."

A Stopgap Kitchen
The kitchen is the one room Michaela plans to overhaul—someday. In the meantime, the existing design has been coaxed into a more-than-palatable guise: its concrete floor was unearthed under linoleum and then polished, and the open shelves were revealed when Michaela removed the cabinet doors. The unifying trick? Paint everything a warm white and stock the shelves with clear glass jars.

01

02

01-03 The Everyday Elevated

When Michaela signs her e-mails
"Live in beauty," she means it. Her
stoneware oil and vinegar bottles
are from a trip to Germany. The
Ferm Living pot holder is knit from
cotton rope (if you have large knitting
needles, you, too, can whip one off).
And a canvas container holds a pot of
exuberant wildflowers.

how to live

I'm made of canvas,
and you can use me as you wish !
let me hold your stuff.
, throw trash in me!
I come in sizes Skinny, Medium, Fat,
Grande, Dice & Pool.

03

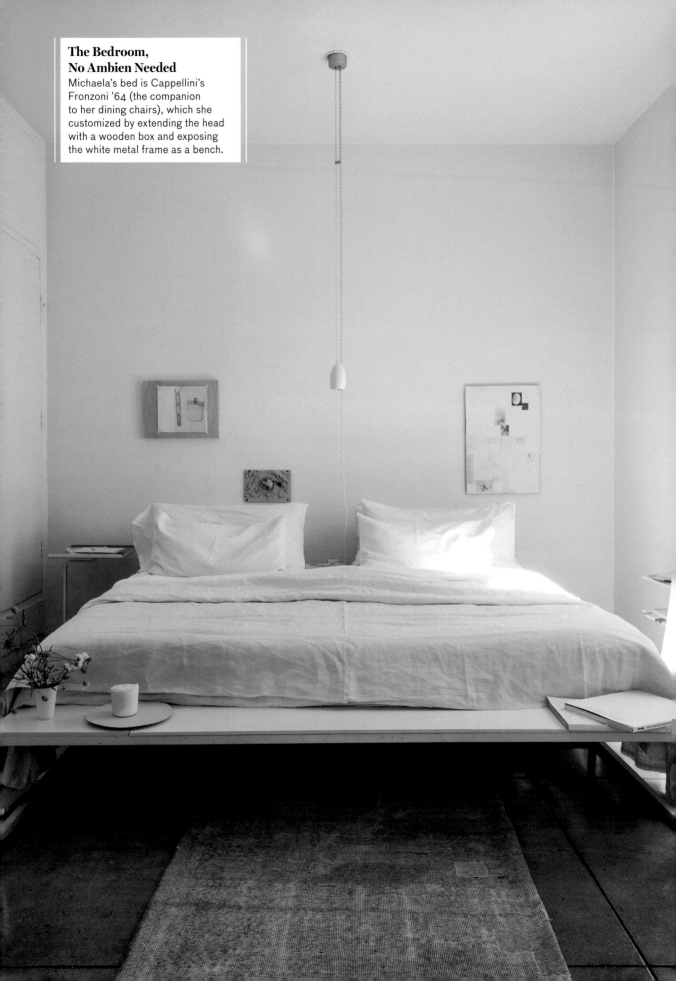

The Bedroom, No Ambien Needed

Michaela's bed is Cappellini's Fronzoni '64 (the companion to her dining chairs), which she customized by extending the head with a wooden box and exposing the white metal frame as a bench.

04

04 The World's Tiniest Spa Bath

Michaela was inspired by a postcard of a sunken bathtub from ancient Crete when she renovated this small bathroom. Using a carefully tinted white concrete ("I wanted it to have an aged feeling, like old stone"), she devised a tub with a minimalist footprint by sinking it below the floor about 18 inches, so that the bather's legs are partly subterranean.

05 Floating Rectangles

The resin sink, by Como, echoes the lines of the tub; Arne Jacobsen's Vola fixtures in matte steel and white-tipped bulbs in porcelain sockets complete the minimalist tableau.

05

Steal This Look

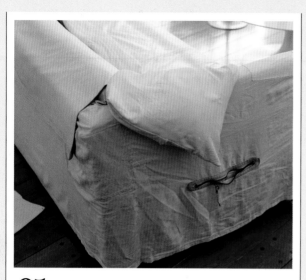

01
The Animal-Proofed Sofa

The living room sofa is layered with a linen slipcover and a white leather blanket, a combination that's both good-looking and practical. The linen serves as protection from cat claws, and the leather as protection from dogs (and visiting children) that jump on everything—it's harder-wearing than linen and can be cleaned off with the swipe of a sponge. Michaela had her leather custom-stitched and held in place with Velcro, though, she points out, you could simply drape and tuck a large hide. A side pocket with an antiqued brass zipper holds the television remote and reading glasses.

02
A TV Inset
Over the Mantel

"You never know what's behind walls," says Michaela, who stole space from an alcove on the back side of her bedroom mantel as a place for the TV. The mantel, formerly painted dark green and rust, is now Shakeresque in its simplicity, which allows for a busy hearth: in addition to a towering stack of magazines, it holds a DVR and a receiver.

03
Books with
Pale Covers

"I love the nuances of different textures and tones and how they play off one another," says Michaela of her penchant for displaying books with blank covers. True, her approach makes it tricky to put a finger on the volume you're after. But it works for aesthetes—and those who know exactly what they've got. In addition to removing book jackets, she turns them inside out, and she sometimes displays books page-side out.

04

Mood Boards as Fine Art

Let others agonize over the right art for their walls. Michaela makes her own using unexpected (but readily available) materials and a technique anyone could master: her canvases are HardieBacker boards—heavy, concrete-colored panels typically used as a base for floor tiles, and available at building supply stores. She layers these with black-and-white photos, printouts, and pictures from design catalogs. To create a permanent collage (and because the boards are too dense for pushpins), she seals the pages in place with an under- and overlayer of Mod Podge. In the examples shown here, architectural views add pattern and depth to a windowless living room wall.

05

Stack Linens on a Rolling Cart

If, like us, you horde lengths of fabric—for tablecloths, future pillows, and just because you like them—chances are you've long ago run out of closet space. Take a tip from Michaela and keep your stash in an old industrial metal cart on wheels, so it needn't always be on view. A cart also works well for corralling tableware collections (see page 280).

The New Old-World Glamour

Remodelista cofounder Francesca Connolly and her family live in a nineteenth-century brownstone that freely crosses the border between historic and contemporary, custom and off-the-shelf, outsized and human-scaled.

ABOVE: Francesca in her front hall.

OPPOSITE: Edith Wharton's New York? Not exactly. With its 14-foot-high ceilings, marble mantel, and man-of-war-shaped chandeliers, the parlor floor telegraphs grandeur. But it's also an inviting place to steal a nap. Francesca and her husband made it architect Steven Harris's mandate to not only restore but also domesticate the formal space. He accomplished the job by paring down the period details and introducing a more modern sensibility. The furniture spans three centuries and was chosen for its human-scaled proportions and comfort. As for the chandeliers, they're vintage Broadway props, selected because, says Steven, "They're theatrical but not too serious. As my mother would say, 'They're chewing gum and baling wire.'"

Francesca Connolly is one of those people born with an impeccable sense of style. She began her career as a textile designer, and her talents extend to creating deceptively simple interiors. She and I have known each other since childhood (our mothers were best friends), and we've been carrying on design-related conversations as long as we both can remember—Francesca influenced by her Italian mother and relatives, me by my Marimekko-minded mother and Swedish grandparents.

Naturally, we've been each other's sounding boards over the course of multiple moves and remodels. In Francesca's case, that's included two overhauls of the 1870 brownstone in Brooklyn Heights where she and her family live. Her husband, Marc, chased the building's owner for years and closed the deal—without ever touring the interior—while Francesca was giving birth to their third child. The structure had been chopped up into nine warren-like apartments in the 1970s, and the couple initially carved out a duplex for the five of them.

Several years later, they set about returning the brownstone to its original state as a single-family house. After interviewing nearly a dozen architects, they hired Steven Harris as well as his partner, Lucien Rees Roberts, an artist and interior designer with his own firm who frequently collaborates with Steven. "Their vision involved the most work," says Francesca, "but it also seemed the most sensible. Steven's a purist and believed strongly in respecting the way the house was originally imagined." That entailed re-creating a classic brownstone front stoop—a feat requiring New York City Landmarks Preservation Commission approval and near-obsolete craftsmanship—while also introducing a high-style galley kitchen on the parlor floor. Francesca and family celebrate the results every day.

01 An Elegant (and Hardworking) Entry

With its clean lines and glam-modernist vibe, the entry introduces the look of the house to come. The Alvar Aalto light is the first of several sculptural fixtures, no two alike. The floor is Azul Atajia limestone, detailed with an inset coir mat. The antiqued mirror isn't just a space enlarger: "Mirrors are perfect in entryways," notes Lucien, "so you can look at yourself before you greet someone or head out." (For details on the oak shelf, see page 174.)

02 Desk as Display Piece

A custom replica of a 1970s Scandinavian design, this rosewood floating desk was envisioned as a living room work space. It evolved into a gallery-like platform, the perfect place to display small paintings and objects in a commanding space.

The Parlor, Improved

The living room's spectacular carved mantel is original, a grande dame surrounded by an audience of glamorous younger and more understated things. The key piece of furniture is an 8-foot-long mohair sofa with a tufted seat. Modeled after a $20,000 midcentury design Francesca spotted in a gallery, it was replicated for much less than that by Brooklyn upholsterers Interiors by George and Martha.

03 A Setting for Dining (and for Doing Homework)

The oak dining table, made from a pair of Florence Knoll bases found on eBay, is where all the family meals take place. And after dinner, it's where the three kids choose to do their schoolwork, a fact that Francesca credits to the supremely comfortable, if unexpected, dining chairs—Eero Saarinen's classic office chair in a wool bouclé as soft as the family's toy poodle.

04 Drilled-Down Glamour

Francesca likes clear counters and isn't encumbered by a houseful of small objects, but she does have a favorite kitchen accessory: an *oliera*, or olive oil decanter, in sterling silver. A wedding present from Italian relatives, it gets prime real estate next to the stove.

04

03

A Modernist Igloo

In her kitchen, Francesca is so clutter-phobic that she thought long and hard before succumbing to an electric mixer. It's no surprise then that expanses of marble—8-inch-by-6-inch custom-cut white Thassos tiles from Ann Sacks on the walls, statuary marble on the counter—make her very happy. Driving home the clean theme, the cabinets are Glacier White Corian, an indestructible material more typically used for counters because it's heavy. To create a feeling of openness, the lower cabinets float off the floor. The room gets plenty of natural light, thanks to one of its most coveted details: a steel-framed glass door that opens to a terrace.

The Cubist Shower

When it came to designing new rooms for the house, including all of the baths, Steven responded to Francesca's minimalist leanings. For the master bath, he created a glass cube shower and an oak sink cabinet against a marble backdrop—pure white Thassos on the walls and Carrara on the floor.

05

05 A Bedroom Straight out of a Dream

Not surprisingly, the ethereal pale blue of the master bedroom took a few tries to get exactly right (the magic formula: Benjamin Moore Glass Slipper cut with 40 percent Benjamin Moore Cloud White). It cloaks the space in a cloud-like haze, accentuated by a movie-star chaise, a velvet-upholstered reproduction from Lost City Arts.

06 Francesca's Quiet Space

Having designed textiles, Francesca understands their power to shape a space. She layers sofas with velvet pillows and cashmere throws. Her beds are quiet symphonies of hue and texture. And in her home office, Margherita, a daisy-patterned rug by her favorite fashion designer, Marni (available from The Rug Co.), brings an otherwise no-nonsense room to life.

07

07 The Smallest Room in the House

A wide window seat is used as a platform for a twin bed. Interrupted by a wall, the wooden ledge gracefully extends from one bedroom to the next (shown below).

08 Jack and the Beanstalk

One end of the window seat has evolved into a thriving plant bay. It originated when Francesca's son started rescuing blossomless orchids that he kept spotting in the trash.

09 The Inspired Teen Lair

Francesca's son applied an inventive hand to the design of his room. Burlap sacks—props from a student movie—hang over his platform bed, which has a floating headboard upholstered in a vintage plaid blanket. The same blanket was used to make oversized pillows for the window seat.

08

09

Steal This Look

01
A Well-Composed Mantel

Francesca has a knack for mantel dressing. Her formula: hang art that you love (here, three lyrical abstract pieces in white frames; the large one is by Elliott Puckett), use candles and votives freely, and accessorize with objects of varying sizes, such as children's clay art and a fistful of flowers.

02
Invisible Entry Storage

A minimalist oak shelf is the quiet lynchpin detail in the entry. Built for the space, it conceals a radiator (which sends heat through vents on the underside) and has a slot drawer that's packed with gloves, hats, sunglasses, and other front hall essentials.

03
Linen-Covered Pinboard

The secret behind the house's orderly look? Fabric-covered bulletin boards in nearly every room for artwork as well as calendars and school notices. Fabricated by an upholsterer, they consist of a section of rolled cork with linen neatly stretched over it and adhered with staples and glue. "The only tricky part," says Lucien, "is getting results that are square and flat."

04
Gorgeous Grilles

Introducing a rare phenomenon: the aesthetically pleasing heating vent. This nickel-plated fish-scale air vent cover was made by Brooklyn-based Architectural Grille (archgrille.com). For something similar, look for a local metal shop that specializes in residential work.

05
Round Coffee Table

Most coffee tables are large and rectangular, but Francesca is an advocate of the small and circular. "They're better for the flow—no sharp corners and they don't anchor you to the couch." Her choice: the Moon table, a patinated steel design with a tarnished mercury glass top from Ochre.

06
Floating Headboard

Each of the children's rooms has a platform bed and a conceptual headboard of sorts; made by an upholsterer, it consists of nothing more than a strip of plywood covered in foam with fabric stapled over it. Get out a staple gun and copy the look yourself, or have an upholsterer do it for you. Francesca's headboards are securely mounted to the walls with large aluminum Z Clips.

Kitchens

Join us for an in-depth look at nine different approaches to the lynchpin room in the house. From the modest galley to the restaurant-style special, each is presented like a recipe, with a plan and a breakdown of the crucial ingredients.

The Formal Eat-In Kitchen

Nearly ten years after a hugely successful remodel of an 1839 Greek Revival town house, actress Julianne Moore decided to airlift the basement kitchen up a flight, placing it on the parlor floor in a space with a dramatic black marble fireplace and 11-foot-tall ceilings. But she wanted her family's gathering place to look as if it belonged there—which is how she ended up with one of the world's most sophisticated, unkitchen-y kitchens.

OWNERS

Julianne Moore and Bart Freundlich

DESIGNER

Oliver Freundlich of Oliver Freundlich Design LLC, New York City

She may be a movie star, but Julianne moonlights as a design junkie. She has exacting standards, worships the spare aesthetic of Belgian architect Vincent Van Duysen, and gravitates to early modernist furniture and homey handmade pottery. Conveniently, her brother-in-law Oliver Freundlich is her favorite architectural designer in town. Her husband, Bart, is a film and television director, as well as the family cook and a huge fan of his wife's and brother's designs—as long as they're practical. "I err on the side of discomfort," says Julianne. "Bart is the voice of reason."

The Plan

Oliver and Julianne set out to insert an eat-in kitchen in her 13-foot-wide, 20-foot-long former living room. The challenge: They wanted the result to be high-functioning without compromising the historic charm of the structure or succumbing to any Betty Crocker moments (i.e., no overhead cabinets, no drawer pulls, no refrigerator on view). Oliver solved the riddle by running a minimalist table down the middle and designating what he terms three "ecosystems" so that what's needed for each task is on hand—and the fridge is in the pantry. "It's a room set up for living rather than for professional cooking," he says.

Countertops

Each work surface is finished with honed black granite. "Typically in kitchens, you see contrasting countertops," says Julianne. "We wanted it all of a piece for a cleaner, more formal look."

Dish Cabinet

Found from an Antwerp dealer on 1stdibs, the midcentury design by Willy Van der Meeren (left) is topped with a movie souvenir, a fiberglass cast of Julianne's body, made to outfit her with prosthetics.

Appliances

La Cornue's Château 120, an oven detailed like a Rolls-Royce, is on full view (opposite); the Bosch dishwasher is disguised behind a wood-paneled door; and the fridge and other appliances are in the adjoining pantry (shown on the following page).

Hood

Julianne dislikes hoods, except when they're plaster—"built into the wall with a sculptural presence." Oliver created a facsimile by enclosing a 48-inch Viking hood behind painted wood casing.

Backsplash

Concrete squares from Mosaic House protect the wall behind the range. Their selling points: they have a matte finish—Julianne is anti-shiny—and are a close tonal match to the wall color.

Cutlery

While filming in Toronto. Julianne read about Mjölk on Remodelista. Between takes, she dashed to the shop and bought her Sori Yanagi flatware.

Cabinetry

Made of blackened, rift-sawn European white oak, all of the cabinetry (shown on previous pages) is freestanding and anchored at waist height. "It's designed to look like furniture with modern reveal detailing and crisp lines," explains Oliver, who added 4-inch-tall recessed toe kicks to make the pieces look as if they're on plinths. Black was chosen to relate to the mantel and window trim. The fact that it all looks so good is thanks, he says, to a very skillful contractor, Jesse Robertson-Tait.

184 | **Storage**

Each work area has built-in cupboards or drawers. Supplies and dry goods are kept in two pantries created from a coat closet and a home office (below). "Having enough storage," says Oliver, "is what enables this setup to work."

Radiators

The kitchen and pantry both have new versions of classic metal radiators that Oliver sourced from British company Bisque. They're in a gunmetal finish called anthracite and are also available in a range of colors. (A caveat: Oliver warns that during shipping, storage, and installation, the radiators can get chipped, so handle with care.)

Wall Treatment

In its previous guise, every room in the house was painted a different shade of gray, but Julianne was ready for something "bright and cleaner." The winner? Benjamin Moore's White Dove. A woman who knows what she likes, Julianne limits the palette in her house to ivory, gray, black, brown, green, and the occasional purple.

Sink and Faucet

Like the counters, the custom sink (shown on page 181) is black granite, paired with a deck-mounted Vola faucet in black.

Furniture

Julianne has been picking up vintage finds for decades. She follows her mother's rule that everything in the house be put to use.

Dining Table: A contemporary take on the farmhouse table, the design is a custom replica of Jasper Morrison's Gamma table. Tailored for the space, it has a 9-foot span (with a concealed honeycomb support system) and no visible struts or rails, so it looks something like a child's drawing of a table (see pages 180–181).

Dining Chairs: "The dealer said they might be Jean-Michel Frank," says Julianne of the 1940s set she shipped home from Paris back in 1995.

Armchair: A Brazilian design bought from the set of the movie *Blindness*, it's draped in a chocolate sheepskin from 3-Corner Field Farm at New York's Union Square farmers' market.

Flooring

The original wide-plank pine, with top nails and divots preserved, was stained a deep walnut to give it, explains Oliver, "a sophisticated vibe vs. a rustic vibe." An old Berber rug found on 1stdibs was added for warmth.

Hardware

Instead of knobs or pulls, the drawers and cabinets have reveal openings. The French door handles are from Bass Securities, a company that makes multipoint locking hardware.

Extra Ingredient

High Art and a Hint of Explorer's Club: Large-scale photographs by Ori Gersht (over the mantel), Jack Pierson (over the sink,) and Nan Goldin (over a console) lend the room the feeling of a salon. A touch of greenery and other natural elements, including a giant sea sponge and a trio of vintage tortoiseshells, set the scene for a room with drama.

The Urban Cabin Kitchen

London-based Plain English modestly calls itself a cupboard maker. In fact, the company is in the business of selling complete kitchens that are handsome, well-crafted updates of designs that a Downton Abbey scullery maid would recognize. Plain English has yet to set up shop Stateside but offers plenty of inspiration from afar. We're particularly taken with the Osea kitchen, its first foray into modernist territory. Named after the wild coastline of Osea Island in Essex, the design makes use of rugged materials—stone, wood, leather—to present a clean-lined yet characterful alternative to today's austere constructions.

DESIGNER

**Katie Fontana, Creative Director,
Plain English Design**

Katie Fontana founded Plain English with Nick Niblock back in 1992. Their work has been hugely influential, and the company counts Prince Charles among its fans. When his Prince's Foundation for the Built Environment created a model eco-friendly, affordable house, Plain English was enlisted to come up with the kitchen.

The Plan

Plain English's counterresponse to the minimalist movement, the kitchen was planned, says Katie, to introduce a "cozy country-in-the-city feel to a contemporary setting." A work island fronts a "cupboard run" containing all of the appliances and a single overhead shelf. There's also a trestle table and a wood-burning stove (hence the shelves of kindling). The overall effect: "Goldilocks and the Three Bears" for sophisticates.

Cabinetry

The cupboard wall has a plywood carcass with a combination of solid poplar and MDF on the exterior, all of it initially painted white and later changed to a bright green by Adam Bray for Papers and Paints Ltd. The lesson: don't be afraid of experimenting with bold colors—after all, you can always repaint.

Island

Built of American poplar, the island is painted Peppercorn, a blue-gray color by Sanderson, and fitted with open oak shelving and screening made of glazed steel.

Countertops

The island has a 2-inch-thick worktop of unpolished Belgian fossil stone—"I like its dusky, slightly raw look," says Katie. She paired it with a solid oak section at one end as a cutting board. The cabinets are topped with Carrara marble, 1 inch thick, a long-standing staple in British kitchens.

Sinks and Faucets

Plain English advocates a wealth of sink options. The two in the island are intended for the bulk of the work—one for washing dishes, the other for drying them—and have deep stainless-steel basins made for commercial use. The small prep sink opposite is, says Katie, "for when someone is monopolizing the main sinks and you want to peel some carrots or fill the teakettle." The faucets—two lab pillar taps, one brass lab bridge mixer—all came from eBay and were introduced "to add a bit of character and fun."

Storage

The island is kitted out with an arsenal of storage options: it has open shelving for tableware, glass-fronted drawers for linens, and pullout divided bins for pantry items. For perishables, such as apples and onions, that don't require refrigeration, it also has slatted drawers, as well as screened cupboards—old-fashioned details that deserve to be rediscovered.

Flooring and Wall Treatments

Pale wood grain and a grid of white tiles fill the space with lively but understated pattern.

Wood: Wide-plank Douglas fir runs from the floors up the cupboard wall, for a log-cabin effect. The boards are from Danish flooring company Dinesen, which supplies a lye-and-soap finish that gets applied every three months and helps the floor stand up to a surprising amount of wear and tear.

Tile: The walls surrounding the kitchen table are sheathed in 4-inch-by-8-inch white subway tiles (below) that extend across a door—without a line off-kilter. Using strips of blackened steel, Plain English built a tiling tray onto the face of the door (factoring in both the width of the tiles and the door). They then cut the tiles to fit and added a vintage handle.

Furniture

Katie designed a collapsible trestle table of Douglas fir and encircled it with three-legged oak stools made by Another Country (shown on page 176).

Extra Ingredient

Eccentric Lighting: Aside from recessed fixtures in the ceiling, the lighting is vintage and refreshingly unorthodox in size and shape. A large lantern hovers over the island, a utilitarian piece translated as contemporary sculpture. And a towering lab light stands like a footman next to the table. These pieces play a strong supporting role in the urban cabin look of the kitchen.

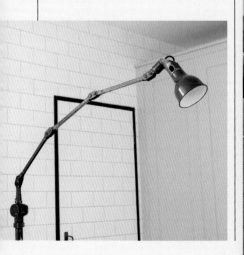

The Long and Lean Kitchen

Removing the back porch of a Victorian town house added 5 feet to the kitchen but resulted in a floor plan reminiscent of a bowling alley. Its owners made masterful use of the proportions by introducing a sleek wood counter on one side and a wall of nearly invisible floor-to-ceiling cabinets on the other.

OWNERS/DESIGNERS
Dagmar Daley and Zak Conway

Dagmar and Zak are both designers with far-reaching résumés. She runs her own children's clothing company, Dagmar Daley, out of a cottage in their backyard. He took six months off from his work as an architect/project manager to do the construction (see their bathroom on pages 246–249).

The Plan

This refreshingly original galley kitchen consists of a long walnut counter opposite a bank of storage cabinets. The wall above the counter is paneled with vertical tongue-and-groove wainscoting and detailed with a narrow display shelf. The space ends in 7-foot-tall custom windows— re-creations of the originals—that surround the family table.

Cabinetry

The walnut counter is seamlessly divided into shelving and drawers. The cupboards (above) have solid-core 8-foot-tall doors and custom pivot hardware that fronts shelving from Ikea.

Storage

Though the kitchen has a streamlined look, it holds a surprising amount of stuff: its cupboards are packed with tableware, beer-making equipment, and inherited porcelain.

Sink and Faucet

The sink is an undermount Blanco in stainless. The Sign of the Crab faucet is by Strom Plumbing and was sourced from Omega Too, in Berkeley, for about $350. The key to the look, says Dagmar, "is to opt for a polished nickel finish and to use a wall-mounted model, which prevents water from building up on the wood countertop."

Appliances

All of the appliances were selected for their small-scale proportions, which the couple feels their narrow kitchen requires. "In this world of appliances on steroids, we did a lot of digging to find what we needed," says Dagmar.

Fridge: An Amana stainless model, found at a used appliance store, was inset in the least visible wall at the sink end of the room.

Dishwasher: A Bosch Integra model (left) was concealed behind a walnut panel for an uninterrupted counter front.

Range: The couple paired a GE Monogram oven with a cooktop by Fisher & Paykel (opposite, below).

Wall Treatment

Dagmar always uses Kelly-Moore Paints' Acoustic White, making it very easy to repaint or touch up.

Flooring

Douglas fir was selected to match the original subfloor exposed elsewhere in the house.

Lighting

A Victorian cast-iron chandelier from antiques store Gypsy Honeymoon is suspended from its original tasseled cord. Its candles are lit "even when we're having takeout," says Dagmar, who grew up with the tradition.

Furniture

Vintage Scandinavian pieces echo the color of the counter and turn the setup into a gathering place.

Dining Table and Chairs: Both are 1960s Danish.

Side Chair: This design (left), by Niels Otto Møller, is available from Design Within Reach.

Bench: Extending off the rosewood counter, the bench is cushioned with grain-sack pillows. Under it, Dagmar keeps two big baskets: one for cookbooks, the other for mail.

Extra Ingredient

Curiosity-cabinet-style displays: Grouped tidily by color and type, Dagmar's collections of lab funnels, Eva Zeisel ceramics, and hotel teapots lend the room an added layer of depth.

The Ultimate Ikea Kitchen

Located in a nineteenth-century barn in upstate New York that was moved to the site and rebuilt using energy-efficient and environmentally conscious materials, the kitchen was almost entirely put together from Ikea parts. The result, however, is unlike any Ikea kitchen we've ever seen.

OWNERS

Jeanette Bronée and Torkil Stavdal

ARCHITECT

Kimberly Peck, New York City

Originally from Denmark and Norway, respectively, Jeanette and Torkil first met at a design event in New York, where they struck up a conversation about kitchens. He's a photographer and also the in-house carpenter; she's a nutritionist with a previous career as an interior designer specializing in fashion showrooms. Architect Kimberly Peck is an expert in stylish sustainable design.

The Plan

The couple wanted a space that would allow them to cook in tandem, each with a sink and a work area. The kitchen overlooks the dining table so that Jeanette can hold classes and host meals in which she demonstrates culinary techniques. Jeanette and Torkil devised the kitchen components with specialists at Ikea; their architect then fine-tuned all of the measurements and drew up the plans—not essential when buying from Ikea, but a good way to ensure that there are no surprises or disappointments during the construction process.

Cabinetry

Jeanette and Torkil worked with kitchen planners at Ikea to pick out the cabinets and drawers. When the units they wanted didn't come in stainless, the Ikea team helped them swap out fronts from other lines to make it work. For their tall pantry cupboards, since stainless wasn't available, they settled on a white-melamine-fronted option.

Hardware

Ikea's U-shaped Attest handles of stainless steel are about $4 for two.

Countertops

Numerär, Ikea's 1½-inch-thick oak butcher block, was chosen for practicality and to offset all the stainless steel.

Storage

Under-the-counter drawers and cabinets are all fitted with dividers to tailor them for glass jars or pot lids or Jeanette's saltcellar collection. Like everyone who owns an Ikea kitchen, Jeanette and Torkil love the way the drawers self-close with a whoosh. Pantry goods are kept alongside the fridge in Ikea pullout shelves.

Sinks and Faucets

"We both love to cook and are often in need of a sink at the same time," explains Jeanette regarding the dual Boholmen stainless sinks from Ikea. As for the Danze Parma Single-Handled Gooseneck faucets: "Ikea's options didn't measure up. I wanted an industrial feel and something that works extremely well."

Backsplash

The tiles are Heath Ceramics' 2-inch-by-6-inch Modern Basics in glossy soft white. "We considered subway tiles, but they get so clinical-looking," says Torkil. "Heath's are handmade and more interesting." The ceramic outlet covers are from Rejuvenation.

Appliances

By sticking with Ikea, and selecting a stainless finish for everything, Jeanette and Torkil created a cohesive unit. Noting that Ikea's appliances are made, but not signed, by Whirlpool, the couple say they've been very happy with their choices.

Refrigerator: The Nutid, a double-door design with a bottom freezer.

Range: The Praktfull PRO A51KS, a five-burner gas oven. No hood or fan needed: "We don't cook meat or greasy stuff," says Jeanette.

Dishwasher: Also from Ikea's Nutid line, it has a clean front (buttons are concealed on the door top) and is so quiet, reports Torkil, that they have to put their ears to it to make sure it's on.

Wall Treatment

Envisioning a textured surface, "like Venetian plaster but not so chi chi," Jeanette had the walls finished with a tinted plaster over Sheetrock.

Furniture

There's no formality needed when you live in a barn, but Torkil and Jeanette like clean-lined shapes.

Dining Table: Restoration Hardware's 1900s Boulangerie Table, modeled after old French designs and made from scaffolding wood.

Dining Chairs: Vintage Danish from CircaModern.com, the couple's favorite source for 1960s Scandinavian furniture at reasonable prices.

Flooring

Polished concrete with radiant heating was chosen for its industrial look, practicality—it warms the house in the winter and keeps it cool in the summer—and durability (the couple has two Rottweilers).

Lighting

Departing from Ikea, Torkil introduced designs that he adapted or invented himself. They ensure that the space looks anything but generic.

Smoky Glass Globes: Torkil swapped out the plastic cords that came with Niche Modern's Solitaire Modern Pendant Light for black cotton-overbraid cord from SundialWire.com, and added tubular filament bulbs, available from Restoration Hardware and Amazon.com.

Hanging Bulb Lights: Torkil made these using the same black cotton-overbraid cord he used on the globe lights, porcelain sockets, and retro-looking teardrop filament bulbs from Restoration Hardware.

LED Light Strip: Another homemade design by Torkil, this is concealed behind a stainless-steel panel atop the back wall tiles (shown opposite, top left). ElementalLED.com sells LED strip lights by the foot.

Extra Ingredient

Hidden Utility: Torkil used Benjamin Moore chalkboard paint on the doors of two kitchen closets that he built, one of which conceals a stacked washer-and-dryer unit.

The Perfect Galley Kitchen

Confronted with a grim old-school galley kitchen and a budget too small to allow for tearing down walls, a young couple and their architect pulled off an extremely practical—and great-looking—overhaul. The secret? A flush facade, thanks to small-scaled European appliances concealed behind paneled doors, and a raised ceiling that allows for sky-high storage cabinets. It adds up to a clean, white, at-your-service space.

OWNERS

Ann DeSaussure Davidson and Scott Davidson

ARCHITECT

Josh Pulver of A + C Architecture + Construction, New York City

Ann is the photo director at *Redbook* magazine; she chronicled the highs and lows of her apartment renovation on her blog, DIYwithADD. Scott is an artist with a tool kit (he was enlisted to make the poplar dividers for the kitchen's cutlery drawer). Architect Josh Pulver specializes in challenging urban renovations.

The Plan

The 75-square-foot galley is designed, as Ann puts it, to have "eye-level lines that are clean and unbroken." The exterior wall contains the sink, appliances, and extratall cabinets. The interior wall has a narrow counter with cupboards below—including an ingenious slot for the microwave—and a pot rack and open shelves above. At the far end of the room, a door leads to an outdoor eating deck.

Cabinetry

Shaker-style and custom-built, the 24-inch-deep wood cabinets (with soft-close doors) rise to the ceiling. The upper reaches contain a trove of inherited silver chafing dishes and mint julep glasses. "A rolling ladder would have come in handy," says Ann, "but a step stool works."

Countertops

Inspired by the original sidewalks in their neighborhood, Ann and Scott selected black cleft slate for their counters, attracted by its color and texture. "Don't be afraid of slate," says Ann. "We put hot pans on it, we spill things on it, and I've dropped a knife on it. A little olive oil or sanding makes any blemish disappear."

Storage

On the wall opposite the cabinets, the 13-inch-deep custom-built cupboards hold pantry goods. The bracketed shelves above them display a lineup of glassware, all of it clear to keep an open look. Pots hang from a steel bar purchased at a restaurant supply store.

Hardware

Ann checked out less expensive look-alikes before deciding that Restoration Hardware's solid brass Aubrey pulls with a satin nickel finish would hold up best for the long haul.

Range: Bertazzoni 30-inch four-burner.

Dishwasher: Bosch.

Microwave: GE (left).

Hood

A discreet exhaust fan is tucked into the ceiling above the range. In addition to not having space for a hood, the couple are vegetarians and say they rarely need a fan. When they do, they open the deck door.

Sink and Faucet

Ann researched the best apron-front sinks for their budget and chose the Belle Forêt Fireclay, which cost close to $800. The Kohler deck-mount bridge faucet (from its Parq series) fills deep pasta pots in seconds and was just under $800 from eFaucets.com.

Backsplash

Having broken the bank on appliances and fixtures, the couple couldn't afford the backsplash tiles they wanted. Instead, they painted their century-old brick wall. Down the line, they can tile

Appliances

Because the space is narrow, the couple shelled out for European appliances that have a shallower profile and can take custom panels. Says Ann, "Our kitchen is the throughway to our deck, so we wanted all of the appliances to be flush with the counters to maximize walking space and minimize hip bruises."

Refrigerator: Liebherr with a bottom freezer (below).

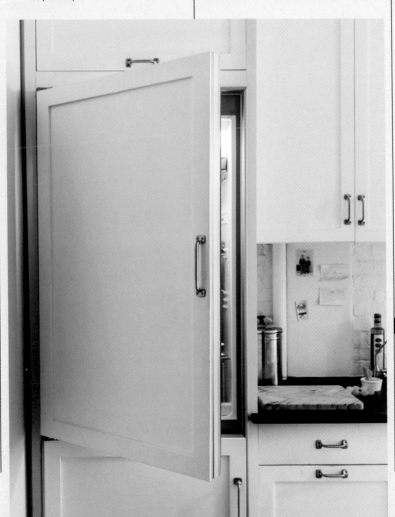

right over it.

Wall and Ceiling Treatments

The main wall and appliance fronts were painted Benjamin Moore Atrium White, while the open shelf wall is Valspar Breath of Blue, from Lowe's. A paneled tongue-and-groove ceiling, with inset lights, introduces a handmade note to the space.

Flooring

The couple used wide-plank pine throughout the apartment. As with the counters, scratches can be spot-sanded and oiled. "We were careful to choose surfaces that look good used, not just when they're pristine," says Ann.

Extra Ingredient

A Way Out: A single-panel glass door now stands in place of an awkward wooden door to the deck. It fills the kitchen with natural light.

The Tiled Kitchen

Handmade blue-and-white cement tiles, a plywood table, and a soffit of salvaged timber lend the Biscuit Film Works' office canteen a residential feel. The down-home materials serve as a giant welcome mat and would work equally well in a private kitchen.

OWNER

Biscuit Film Works

ARCHITECTS

**Mark Hershman and Erik Schonsett
of Shubin + Donaldson, Los Angeles**

Biscuit is a busy film production company specializing in commercials and music videos with headquarters in Los Angeles and London. Southern California architecture firm Shubin + Donaldson is known for its inventive design solutions.

The Plan

Conceived as "a factory for creating things," the room has a wall of restaurant components and a communal table. It's the colors and patterns that turn an interesting-but-straightforward setup into an exciting—and inviting—one.

Cabinetry and Shelving

Practical stainless-steel fittings (right) were custom-made for the space by local commercial kitchen manufacturer Duray. Wooden trivets on the shelves hold white ceramics and clear glassware—all from Ikea—that work, rather than compete, with the tiles.

Countertops

Gray-veined Carrara marble lends a stateliness to the space.

Appliances

The choice of stainless steel for appliances large and small allows them to visually recede as a unit. Most were sourced from Los Angeles restaurant supply store Surfas.

Dishwasher: Fisher & Paykel's bowed-front double-drawer model fits well into the stainless-steel bank.

Refrigerator: A double-doored commercial model made by True Manufacturing, it echoes the lines of the adjoining cabinets.

Sink and Faucet

The stainless-steel sink was made for the space by Duray. The Elkay gooseneck faucet came from Surfas.

Lighting

Two Caravaggio metal pendant lights (see "The Remodelista 100," page 314) are suspended over the table from their signature red cords.

Windows

Walls of steel-framed windows are used like vertical skylights on two sides of the room. Outfitted with reeded glass, they allow in light while blocking distracting views.

Furniture

The table was custom-made from plywood with exposed bolts. It's a look that can be easily replicated using Burro Brand's birch plywood sawhorses as table legs—they're available on Amazon.com for less than $60 a pair—with a sheet of multilayered, well-grained plywood. The steel stools are modern classics by Bay Area designer Jeff Covey, available directly through his workroom, at CoveyStudio.com.

Flooring and Wall Treatments

Contrasting patterns and textures give the space dynamism.

Tile: The floor and main wall are patterned with Fez encaustic cement tiles from Granada Tiles in Los Angeles. Finished with a matte sealant, they require only soap-and-water mopping. Using the same tiles on the floor and walls creates an immersive effect, and can be done with any tiles.

Wood: To introduce warmth alongside the tiles and stainless steel, the soffit above the counter wall (shown opposite, bottom left) is clad in salvaged wood. Supplied by Elmwood Reclaimed Timber of Kansas City, it's the company's Rocky Mountain Mosaic, a mix it describes as "time-worn planks sun drenched with patina so deep it glows."

Extra Ingredient

No Puzzle Piece out of Place: From the dish soap (contained in a clear glass bottle) and natural scrub brushes to the stainless-steel outlet plates, every detail in this kitchen looks good—a feat for a much-used communal space.

The Tiled Kitchen

A User's Guide to Kitchens

The State-of-the-Art Loft Kitchen

The challenge: to come up with a kitchen that's at once sophisticated, suited to a young family, and unobtrusive (it's exposed to the whole living space). The solution: clean white cabinetry with hidden corners for essentials like the kids' weekly calendar, and a gathering spot in the form of a wooden island that the architects designed to "feel more like a piece of furniture than a kitchen."

OWNERS

James and Bianca Jebbia

ARCHITECTS

**Solveig Fernlund and Neil Logan
of Fernlund + Logan, New York City**

James is the owner of Supreme Skateboards, a brand that has taken skateboard culture to new heights of cool. Bianca worked with her husband for many years, and then went on to jobs at Marni and Prada. They now have two kids, a Chihuahua, and a supremely nice apartment (see their bathrooms on pages 250–253), thanks to husband-and-wife architecture firm Fernlund + Logan.

The Plan

The architects set out to create a minimalist kitchen separated from the rest of the living space by a statuesque island. All of the cabinetry and appliances, down to the wire dish drainer and wooden bread box, were made by Bulthaup, a German manufacturer of modular kitchen systems. Much like Ikea, the company offers a range of fully conceived, ready-to-be-tailored kitchen designs, but Bulthaup stands at the top end of the clean-lined luxury spectrum.

Cabinetry

Bulthaup specializes in what it calls "graphic conciseness," demonstrated here by two streamlined banks of cabinets, under and over the counter. Selected from Bulthaup's b3 kitchen system, the cabinetry is birch fronted by white laminate with white edging.

Storage

The cabinet drawers have "angled ergonomic recessed grips" and are fully loaded with custom dividers. A cupboard opens to reveal a cantilevered pullout that makes great use of corner storage space.

Island

To divide the kitchen from the dining and living area, and to inject some warmth into the all-white setup, Solveig and Neil designed an island of white oak with a clear matte finish. The stools are from Bulthaup.

Countertops

The architects specified stainless-steel counters with a very thin beveled edge, something Bulthaup was able to deliver.

Shelving

Lacquered birch shelves designed by Alvar Aalto and made by Artek display the couple's collection of Picasso ceramics gathered over the years from auctions at Christie's and Phillips.

Appliances

Bulthaup specializes in making appliance-concealing cabinetry; it also sells appliances by Sub-Zero and other brands—making it very easy for the Jebbias to get state-of-the-art equipment.

Refrigerator: 27-inch-wide Sub-Zero 700TCI with two freezer drawers. An under-the-counter Sub-Zero 700BR is used for overflow.

Cooktop: Italian-made gas cooktop by Foster with stainless controls.

Range: Miele H4882BP 30-inch (since discontinued), a computerized design that stores and displays recipes on the black glass door.

Dishwasher: Miele G2472SCVi with a concealed control panel and a divided top tray for cutlery.

Sinks and Faucet

Two 17.70-inch stainless-steel inset sinks by Bulthaup share Bulthaup's signature crooked mixer faucet.

Backsplash

Bulthaup didn't offer what the architects considered a simple-enough backsplash, so they designed one. Made of white-enameled steel, it ends in a narrow shelf running between the counter and the overhead cabinets.

Lighting

The ceiling lights are Elliptipar halogens, and the fanciful coconut chandelier is by New York artist duo Guyton\Walker.

Wall Treatment

The entire loft is painted Benjamin Moore Decorator's White.

Flooring

The Douglas fir floorboards, from Danish flooring company Dinesen, were lightened with lye and are treated every two weeks with Dinesen's special soap, which leaves a soft finish and builds a protective surface. "Having a floor like this is challenging," says Bianca. "When something spills, we drop to our knees in a second with Clorox wipes. But it looks and feels great, and having so much floor space is great in the city—our kids ride their bikes and scooters inside."

Furniture

In such a wide-open, spare setting, every piece has a big impact. The Jebbias chose modern classics that are at home in the limelight.

Dining Table and Chairs: Jean Prouvé's celebrated EM table and painted metal and plywood Standard chairs are both 1950s designs still in production.

The Kids' Table: Offi's circular Chalkboard Table (with an inset bowl for chalk) is paired with its Look-Me Chairs of molded birch ply.

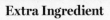

Extra Ingredient

Subtle Wall Outlets: Sourced from Vancouver-based lighting and design company Bocci, they're designed to be mounted flush into the wall so that no cover plate is needed.

The Plan

Sarah set out to remove the granite counter and linoleum floor from sight—without touching them. Having lived for a time in Tokyo, she adopted a Japanese solution: she wrapped them. A freestanding maple counter now sits over the granite, and painted oak floorboards rest atop the linoleum.

The Reinvented Rental Kitchen

"The hardest part of living in our rental was the kitchen," says Remodelista cofounder Sarah Lonsdale, who liked the bones of the U-shaped room well enough, but not its speckled granite counters and sheet linoleum floor. "I long fantasized about covering the counters in stainless steel but couldn't justify the expense." Finally, she gave herself a week and, with help from her husband, David, pulled off a remarkable—and inexpensive—makeover.

RENTERS

Sarah Lonsdale and David Knudsen

Sarah, a survivor of three house renovations and one ground-up construction (her father is an architect), joined Remodelista minutes after its inception. She and David, who works in financial software, decided to leave San Francisco and move to Napa Valley with their two kids to give rural living a try. They initially leased their 1930s cottage for a year. That was in 2006, and they're still happily ensconced. Along the way, without introducing any permanent changes, they have very much made the place their own.

Countertops

It took some trial and error, but North Bay Plywood in Napa was able to fabricate a shell of a counter at a reasonable price ($400 for the wood and custom cutting). After fitting the four ¾-inch maple sections into place, Sarah used a water-based protective finish on both the top and underside around the sink, and applied a clear silicone sealant around the basin. She treated the rest of the counter with walnut oil (which, unlike other vegetable oils, doesn't go rancid), and declared the counter done.

Hardware

Well before Sarah tackled her kitchen's big problems, she had swapped out the existing shiny Ikea knobs for Valli & Valli solid brass knobs with a satin nickel finish (opposite, center)—an easy fix, and an inexpensive way to upgrade a kitchen.

Wall Treatment

Standard white rectangular tile—likely sourced at Home Depot—provides a backsplash and clean-looking walls. The white walls and cabinets were painted by the landlord.

Flooring

The biggest challenge in covering the linoleum was that the wood needed to be thin enough to allow the kitchen doors to open. The other challenge: it had to be untreated oak, because Sarah planned to paint it. Thanks to Donald Williams Wood Floors, in Calistoga, California (and with the help of David's power saw), she painted and then assembled the ½-inch-by-2-inch tongue-and-groove boards. So far, without any added nails, the floor is holding together. And the paint—a coat of Benjamin Moore Silver Gray that allows the grain to show through—provides the understated Scandinavian look Sarah was after. Rather than adding a sealant, she plans to let it wear and to repaint as needed.

Extra Ingredient

Pot Rack: Initially, Sarah didn't like the slatted wood rack (shown on page 222) that came with the kitchen. It's since proven indispensable, not only for storing pots but also for drying herbs and homemade linguine. Kegworks.com sells a similar design.

The California King-Sized Kitchen

When she recently downsized to a 1949 house with all of its original details, interior designer Amanda Pays left most of the rooms as is but introduced a new kitchen scaled to fit her crew (her four sons are all in the vicinity of 6 foot 4). The space is not only an ideal family hub, but also a model of upcycled design. An avid flea market shopper, Amanda subscribes to what she calls the "recycle, restore, and reuse school of remodeling."

OWNERS/DESIGNERS

Amanda Pays and Corbin Bernsen

Amanda Pays is an actress and a serial remodeler who five years ago officially shifted roles and became an interior designer. She and her husband—actor, writer, and director Corbin Bernsen— have four boys, ages fourteen to twenty-three. Amanda designed the kitchen herself but credits her husband with devising a lot of the spatial solutions throughout the house. In lieu of an architect, she worked directly with a draftsman and a contractor.

The Plan

Tailored for a busy family, the 500-square-foot kitchen is versatile enough to serve as the setting for both breakfasts on the run and sprawling dinner parties. To make it work, Amanda established five discrete territories within the room, centered around an L-shaped counter. The oak table has made many moves with the family since Amanda shipped it from England to California in 1994: "That table is the centerpiece wherever we go."

Hardware

The metal cabinet pulls were purchased at a swap meet, a bag of fifty for $25.

Sink and Faucet

Amanda wanted a roomy ceramic sink and likes the fact that Shaws Sinks has been turning out their Original Fireclay apron-front designs since 1897. She chose the Danze Parma Single-Handled Gooseneck faucet in stainless for its "affordability and simplicity: not too shiny or too much going on."

Appliances

While Amanda was pulling together the kitchen, she was also finishing a kitchen for her mother, so she was able to buy appliances in bulk at Sears. The fridge and dishwashers are Kenmore Pro (a nice-looking and lower-priced alternative to Sub-Zero). The stove is Jenn-Air, with a hood that Amanda designed.

Storage

The kitchen is loaded with cabinets and drawers. Pantry items go in a painted cupboard, a long-ago Rose Bowl Flea Market find.

Cabinetry

At Maidera Furniture, reclaimed lumber specialists in Van Nuys, California, Amanda spotted the remains of a barn from Brazil. She used the wood (all of it peroba) to build the cabinetry, ceiling beams, and lintels. Some of the upper cabinets have chicken-wire safety glass, a material found in the room's skylights.

Countertops and Flooring

Matte-finished concrete—durable and suitable for a room with a barnyard vibe—is Amanda's material of choice: "I don't care if kids come in with dripping swimsuits on." As for the counters, she's okay with the way they've become worn and stained: "Concrete is definitely not for the uptight perfectionist, but I like the way it makes the room feel lived in."

Shelving

The bracketed shelves over the stove were built from old scaffolding boards, purchased from the contractor for $10 each.

Furniture

Amanda turned a ragtag mix of vintage finds into a pulled-together ensemble.

Dining Table: An antique purchased at a shop in Farnham, England, it's had many incarnations: Amanda has stripped it and stained it, and then stripped it again before adding the pale wash it has now.

Dining Chairs: The vintage metal institutional chairs were bought on sale at ABC Carpet & Home for $95 each.

Stools: At swap meets, Amanda is always on the lookout for work stools and never pays more than $15 apiece. Despite slightly varying heights and patinas, they work well together.

Work Island

A pair of toolshed tables from the Rose Bowl Flea Market forms the base of a chef's-style workstation, with an added stainless-steel top (shown on page 226).

Wall and Ceiling Treatments

To soften the room and "bring down the height," Amanda introduced a beamed ceiling and fitted it with 6-inch-wide tongue-and-groove paneling. It's painted the same color, Sydney Harbour Paint Company's Plaster of Paris white, as the walls. The 8-inch-by-8-inch concrete tiles on the stove wall complement the gray concrete and white cabinetry. Amanda found them at Badia Design, a Moroccan imports store in North Hollywood.

Lighting

The room has three steel-framed rectangular skylights at the far end, unearthed original features of the house. There are also inset ceiling lights and fanciful suspended lights made from metal chicken feeders. Amanda found them, as well as a pair of bread pan sconces, at Los Angeles warehouse Big Daddy's Antiques.

Extra Ingredient

Retro Doors: A pair of 1940s metal-framed glass doors (left) from Olde Good Things in Los Angeles opens the kitchen to the backyard and pool.

Bathrooms

*Here we explore and explain five standouts,
from our favorite powder rooms to a romantic
Scandinavian master bath unlike any other.*

The Romantic Bath, Frills Allowed

A stylist committed to a Scandinavian aesthetic, Tiina Laakkonen created this dreamy, unabashedly florid master bath for herself and her husband, who was her design collaborator and supervised construction. They envisioned it as a place for the two of them to catch up at the end of the day.

OWNERS/DESIGNERS
Tiina Laakkonen and Jon Rosen
(see their house on pages 30–45)
ARCHITECTS
**Nandini Bagchee of Bagchee Architects and Tim Furzer,
New York City**

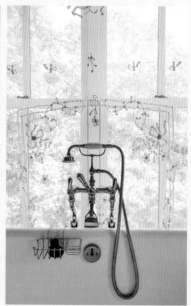

Flooring

The bathroom features a carpet of concrete tiles from French company Carocim, handmade using traditional Moroccan techniques. Tiina had one of her architects create a CAD tile drawing of the floor, and using it, she devised the geometric design on her computer (she did this for each of her bathrooms, all of which feature the same tiles in different patterns). Because of tile breakage, Tiina advises over-ordering by 10 percent.

Wall Treatment

The room is sheathed with 8-inch-wide poplar shiplap, which consists of rabbeted pieces of wood that are fitted together like pieces of a jigsaw puzzle. The work of a master carpenter, the paneling presents a stripped-down, modernist take on classic barn interiors. It's painted a warm white—White Dove from Benjamin Moore's Aura line. For subtle signs of handwork, the couple had the paint applied with a brush rather than a roller.

Window Treatments

In lieu of shades, Tiina hung diaphanous bedspreads in the windows. She bought old-fashioned Italian designs made of cotton netting and Battenburg lace at a flea market in Buenos Aires (you can find examples for about $125 on eBay) and used rings with clips to suspend them from Pottery Barn curtain rods. The results add privacy to the room, as well as a touch of femininity and a steady supply of sunlight.

Bathtub

Kallista's Circe, a cast-iron neo-Victorian design with eagle-claw feet, comes with an enameled interior and an exterior primed for painting. To give it weight against the windows and floor, Tiina and Jon opted to finish it with a black enamel. The deck-mounted nickel faucet and hand shower is from Rohl. A metal stool from a local antiques store serves as a side table and a period companion to the tub.

Sinks and Faucet

For a clean, classic look, Tiina and Jon used Shaws Original pedestal sinks with polished-nickel Rohl fixtures. Nickel has a soft hazy sheen that's far less strident than stainless (and considerably more expensive).

Medicine Cabinets

Wanting cabinets that looked of a piece with the shiplap walls, Tiina and Jon had framed, recessed designs custom made to their specs. A Restoration Hardware glass-shelved étagère between the sinks provides additional storage.

Lights

For understated but ample lighting, Swedish capsule-shaped sconces—a vintage design still in production that Tiina hopes to sell in her shop—light the sink wall, one on each end and a pair in the middle.

Open Storage

The front wall of the shower was extended to create inset shelves (below, far left) for towels, sheets, and art in black and white. Having worked in fashion for decades, Tiina understands the graphic power of sticking to a simple palette. A restored medical cabinet holds toiletries.

Shower

Classic Field tiles from Heath Ceramics create a subtly undulating pattern on the shower walls and floor. "I love their handmade quality," says Tiina. The rain showerhead is from Rohl. The towel hooks are from a mom-and-pop hardware store in Finland.

Extra Ingredient

Outsized Armchair: A comfy classic (from Restoration Hardware) that you'd typically see in a living room, it's positioned in a corner next to the tub, so that while one person bathes, the other can veg out.

The Romantic Bath, Frills Allowed

The Attic Bath

In a 1901 five-story town house, architects
Solveig Fernlund and Neil Logan saw the roofline as an
opportunity to reinvent the old-world garret bath.
"We wanted it to have the feeling of being tucked away,"
notes Neil. The original arched window, a
landmarked feature of the house, was carefully restored
and the sloping walls around it entirely paneled.
The result is a stripped-down version of a
nineteenth-century room that stands out for its
workmanship and lovely sense of restraint.

OWNERS
Jakob Trollbäck and Lisa Smith Trollbäck
ARCHITECTS
**Solveig Fernlund and Neil Logan of Fernlund + Logan,
New York City**

Bathtub

The architects put an enameled steel design by German company Kaldewei to unorthodox use: the Centro Duo Oval 127 is made to be deck-mounted (built-in), but they liked the skeletal look of its legs. After painting the black exterior white, they left the tub exposed.

Sink and Faucet

The sink is a Duravit Vero wall-mounted washbasin, a European classic available in a range of sizes and configurations. The faucet is a Vola HV1 mixer tap in satin chrome.

Medicine Cabinet

The NuTone Metro surface-mount medicine cabinet is a Fernlund + Logan favorite because it's available frame-less and comes in different sizes. It's sold off the shelf for about $250.

Toilet

The architects like the clean geometry of the Duravit Happy D tank toilet and use it in most of their bathrooms.

Flooring

The designers chose to paint the oak floor (Benjamin Moore's Porch & Floor urethane alkyd enamel in Platinum) because furniture stands out so well against it. It has a radiant heating system, so they had to use best-grade oak to prevent it from warping.

Lighting

A porcelain socket, like the one over the mirror, is a $3 item that can none-theless be hard to find in the right size and profile. This one came from Lendy Electric, in Manhattan.

Wall and Ceiling Treatment

The walls, ceiling, and alcove around the window are paneled in paint-grade wood boards (3½ inches wide and ½ inch thick). They're painted with two coats of Benjamin Moore primer and three coats of Benjamin Moore Satin Impervo Enamel in White Dove. The effect is a lesson in the merits of mixing geometry and the Scandinavian palette.

Furniture

The slatted teak table's undershelf is perfect for storing towels. It's paired with a Danish chair by Finn Juhl.

Extra Ingredient

Inventive Vents: No metal plates or grilles necessary. The room's air-conditioning vents (shown on page 232) are rows of holes drilled into the ceiling paneling, one of Fernlund & Logan's signature design details.

The Patchwork Powder Room

A tiny bathroom in a backyard home office is as colorful and varied as the garden it's surrounded by, thanks to Moroccan cement encaustic tiles. Patterned in a kaleidoscope of colors and designs, from foliage to frogs, they blanket the floors, walls, and anteroom.

OWNERS

Michelle McKenna and Brenlen Jinkens

(see their house on pages 122–137)

ARCHITECT

Rahesh Ram of Naau Architecture, London

Sink and Faucet

Made for a lab, the small ceramic sink was sourced from Edward Haes, an antiques dealer specializing in reclaimed parts. It's mounted on teak brackets, which were also used to make a soap dish shelf. The faucet is a stag head in brass, designed by Agnes Emery of Emery et Cie, maker of the room's tiles.

Mirror

Michelle filled in the blanks in her house, including the need for a charming powder room mirror, by shopping at Vintage Heaven, her friend Margaret's booth at the Columbia Road Flower Market, held on Sundays in London's East End. The frame is neatly edged in Japanese washi tape. "The edges of the mirror are beveled, which from a feng shui perspective is not great," explains Michelle. "The tape was an easy solution to the issue."

Storage

To add to the room's handmade details, Michelle had her contractor build a beadboard cabinet over the toilet. She selected simple brass knobs to work with the room's other brass accents.

Toilet

The toilet is from Dorset Reclamation, an architectural salvage yard in Dorset, England. Since it didn't come with a seat, Michelle added one made of oak, both for looks and for comfort.

Wall Treatment and Flooring

A decorative-arts adventurer, Michelle came up with the patchwork idea when she discovered that Belgian company Emery et Cie sells tile remainders in odd lots. "You get what you get," she says. "I ordered extra so I would be able to pick the designs I liked best." In London, the company has a showroom at the design and architectural salvage warehouse Retrouvius. As of yet, there's no U.S. outpost, but worldwide shipping is available (see EmeryEtCie.com).

Extra Ingredient

Towel Warmer: The Victorian-style heated rack is a bathroom luxury ready for a comeback. Michelle sourced her brass model from U.K. towel radiator specialists Maybrays.co.uk.

The New Old Bathroom

Dagmar Daley and Zak Conway transformed what was a fifties galley bathroom into a fresh retro-industrial design by adding wainscoting and reclaimed fixtures that look original—only more interesting.

OWNERS/DESIGNERS
Dagmar Daley and Zak Conway
(see their kitchen on pages 192–197)

Medicine Cabinet

Dagmar and Zak converted a glass-fronted fire extinguisher cabinet into a medicine cabinet by inserting three glass shelves. An extendable two-sided mirror hangs next to it.

Lighting

A dentist's office wall light, found at a garage sale, shines over the sink.

Wall Treatments

The room's pine tongue-and-groove wainscoting was inspired by the paneling in old grocery stores. It's painted with Kelly-Moore Paints' Acoustic White.

Bathtub

The vintage claw-foot tub with its nickel fixtures was given to the couple by a client who was getting rid of it. In order to make the shower curtain less intrusive, they hung it on 30-inch-long ball chains that operate on a hospital track. "I came up with this because I don't like the way tub shower curtains can take up the whole room," says Dagmar. "I also hate it when they get on your skin." Her dropped design prevents both crimes. To buy parts to re-create the look, see HospitalTrackSystem.com

Sink and Faucet

The set was found at Omega, a salvage yard in Berkeley.

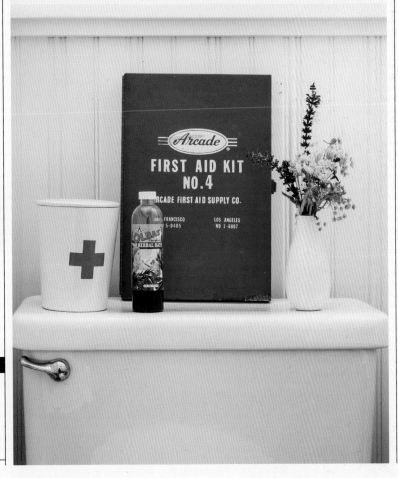

Flooring

The old-fashioned-looking black linoleum is Forbo Flooring Systems' Marmoleum, which is made from natural ingredients, such as linseed oil. It's durable and warm to the touch.

Extra Ingredient

Eye-Catching Props: A Dagmar Daley children's vest, fresh flowers, and other fun-to-look-at objects add life to the quietly spirited room.

Botanicals in the Bath

In the tiny powder room and the master bath of a newly
renovated New York loft, Carrara marble and flora were
used to create enchanting, immersive environments.
By offsetting hard-edged materials with digitally produced
botanical wallpaper and discreet bouquets, the architects
came up with a formula that's at once masculine
and feminine, rigorous but not too serious,
peaceful and entirely uplifting.

OWNERS

James and Bianca Jebbia
(see their kitchen on pages 216–221)

ARCHITECTS

**Solveig Fernlund and Neil Logan of Fernlund + Logan,
New York City**

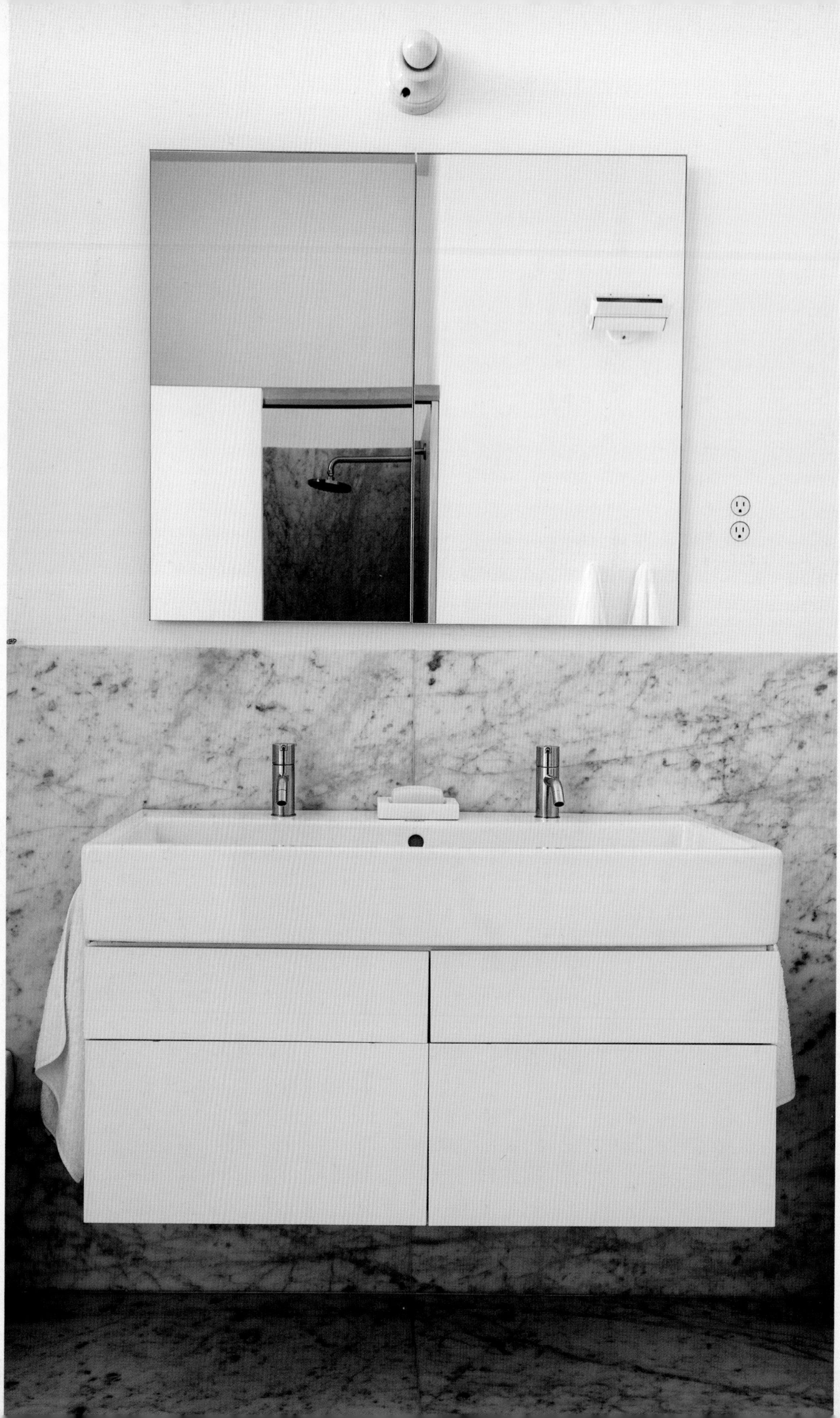

Sinks and Faucets

Solveig and Neil chose Duravit Vero wall-mounted washbasins, with Vola HV1 mixer faucets in satin chrome, which they installed over custom-made consoles of lacquered wood.

Mirrors

The powder room has a beaded silver design likely made for a ship. The master bath's double-doored medicine cabinet was custom-made.

Bathtub

Urban Archaeology's white marble City Bathtub is modeled after an 1890s American design. It weighs over 1,400 pounds.

Toilets

The Duravit Happy D tank toilet was selected for its clean lines (it forms a D shape) and compactness.

Shower

The shower is clad in ¾-inch honed Carrara marble, hand-picked at the stone yard. It has an inset niche lined in the same marble (giving the effect of having been chiseled out of one extrathick slab). The showerhead is by Hansgrohe and the fixture is by Vola.

Wall Treatment

Unlike handmade wallpapers, the one in the powder room is washable and suitable for even high-traffic areas. The pattern, Coastal Plants by Maharam (left), is part of the textile company's digital projects series of artist- and designer-made wallpapers, which Solveig helped produce. It's made to order and sized and priced on a project-specific basis.

Flooring

In both baths, ¾-inch-wide honed Carrara marble was used on the floor and as a graceful baseboard. The same Carrara serves as the backdrop for the toilet and sink—it rises to form a backsplash and a shallow shelf. And along the bath wall, a cutout niche is just big enough to hold a soap dish and two hydrangea blossoms.

Extra Ingredient

Colorful Hamper: A coiled basket woven by Wolof women in Senegal subtly nods to the room's pastel floral theme. For similar designs, see Swahili-Imports.com.

Design Ideas

Too often DIY is TMT—too much trouble.
But not when it comes to these projects. We've
divided the chapter into three sections:
New Uses for Familiar Things (objects with an
inspired twist), Minimum Assembly Required
(for the handy and not-so-handy among us), and
Where's the Stuff? (an exploration of storage).
Get ready to make things happen.

PART 1

New Uses for Familiar Things

Clever recasts. The good news: you might have to do some shopping to pull off these transformations, but there's no gluing or hammering required.

01

Shoe Bag as Plant Holder

Designer Michaela Scherrer frequently uses orchids in her projects and has come up with inventive ways to display them. Sometimes she turns the paper bag they arrive in inside out, spray-paints it white, and cloaks the pot in that. Here, she uses a cotton bag that came with a pair of shoes to create a sack for disguising a plastic pot (and she notes that it would be easy to stitch a facsimile bag in seconds).

02

Jars as Party Glassware

This Depression-era trick has been supplanted by manufactured beakers made to look like mason jars. Our friend Catherine Dann advocates rediscovering the real thing: the jelly jars and honey pots destined for your recycling bin. They make sturdy glasses, and for a party, they're far preferable to disposable cups. Their variety lends a sense of fun and helps everyone keep track of his or her own drink.

New Uses for Familiar Things

Design Ideas

03

Felt as Still Life Anchor

Stylist and furniture designer Scott Newkirk's far-ranging assemblages incorporate Japanese and Roseville ceramics, small landscapes, driftwood, and old snapshots as if they were born to be together. One of his tricks: when arranging art and objects on a tabletop, he includes a washed rectangle of black or gray wool felt as a base layer, to define a surface and "soften up the look."

Ribbon as Door Pull

Hard-pressed to find the right replacement for a missing knob? Follow designer Corinne Gilbert's example: slip a piece of grosgrain ribbon through the door plate and anchor it with a silver bell.

New Uses for Familiar Things

Design Ideas

05

Empty Picture Frames as Shelf Tableaus

Justine Hand has a talent for creating soulful still lifes, and the secret to her displays is often a wood frame. Kept empty, it gives the space and objects around it definition, and invites the eye to fill in the blanks.

06

Dining Table as Desk

Don't feel boxed in by furniture made for a particular purpose. Case in point: dining tables make excellent desks—and not only in executive suites. This one in Miranda Heller's Cape Cod barn is Crate & Barrel's Big Sur design (used as a dining table on page 83). Here, it's paired with a George Nelson bubble lamp, another classic, more commonly hung over a sofa or dining table.

07

Mirror as Vase Coaster

On a bedside table in her barn bedroom, Miranda Heller positioned a pitcher on an antique mirror. Paired with a mercury glass light and silver-gilt frame, these shiny accents act as sun extenders. The painting is by Miranda's aunt Susannah Phillips.

08

Straight-from-the-Bolt Fabric as Curtains

Some people agonize over how to cover their windows. Others, like Miranda Heller, take the easy route: they make their own designs in a matter of minutes. For her bedroom, she bought rough linen yardage and simply snipped it to size, clipped on wooden curtain rings, and looped them through a hardware store dowel.

09

Vintage First-Aid Boxes as Wall-Mounted Bathroom Storage

In addition to having evocative old graphics, tin first-aid boxes come in a range of sizes and colors and are designed to be hung on a wall—all of which makes them ideal as bathroom cabinets. And they're not hard to find or expensive: Catherine Dann found her collection, above, at rummage sales and on Etsy.

10

Flexible Tape as Picture Frames

Scott Newkirk uses artist's tape and see-through plastic covers from art-supply stores to create an ever-evolving display on his bedroom wall. Removable Japanese washi tape also works well for making ad hoc frames.

11

Clipboards as Bulletin Boards

Classic clipboards are still standard issue at office suppliers. Hung from nails on a wall, as Sarah Lonsdale has done here in her home office, they're ideal for gathering papers and take up very little space. We've also admired clipboards used as wall frames. They look especially good painted black and hung in a group, and there's no commitment: you can swap out the art as often as you like.

12

Airline Drinks Trolley as Party Bar

Catherine Dann is a champion hostess who keeps a 1960 Air Algérie bar cart parked in her dining room. Sourced on eBay, it's a feat of compact design that's often put to work: "I can roll around the cart and make drinks, serve hors d'oeuvres, and grab cold bottles, and never leave my guests," says Catherine. Airline swizzle sticks available on request.

New Uses for Familiar Things

Design Ideas

PART 2

Minimum Assembly Required

Willing to do a bit of measuring and hammering—
or to get someone to do it for you? Here, our
best ideas for quickly transforming a room, ranging
from easy to (slightly) complex.

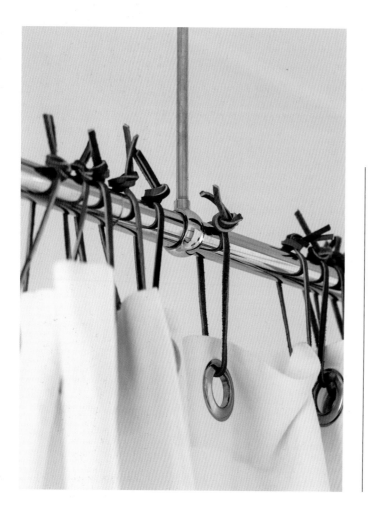

01

Rawhide Shower Curtain Rings

Sarah Lonsdale finds myriad uses for leather laces—as napkin rings, as gift ties, and as drawer pulls in her dining room's built-in sideboard. In her bathroom, she replaced plastic shower curtain rings with 16-inch lengths of knotted leather cord that add a touch of color and texture to the white room. Buy rawhide at your local hardware store or through Amazon.com.

02

Rustic Laundry Hamper

A lidded wooden box makes an ideal dirty clothes bin. Designer Amanda Pays dragged this one home from a swap meet and left the exterior as is. Inside, she added simple metal hooks for suspending two laundry bags (his and hers or dark and light).

03

Whiteboard Wall

A bright-looking alternative to a chalkboard: a whiteboard, painted directly on a wall using dry-erase paint. No need to confine whiteboard walls to offices—they also come in handy in kitchens as places to compile grocery lists and reminders. Here, in designer Michaela Scherrer's kitchen, a vertical joist between French doors has been given a whiteboard band and a hook for market bags.

04

Workstead's Plank Bench

This rustic perch made by architect Robert Highsmith of Workstead is nothing but a balancing act. It consists of a slab of live-edge pine (available to order from most lumber mills) that rests atop a pair of folding metal camp stools. Robert whittled the towel hooks from tree branches.

05

Shelf as Bedside Table

Bedside tables often take up precious space without delivering much in the way of storage. Simplify the setup with a small shelf. This example, designed by actor Corbin Bernsen for his sons' bunkhouse, is made using scaffolding wood (finished with a matte sealer) and steel L brackets.

06

Spatter-Painted Floors

Justine Hand's Cape Cod cottage has several charming old spattered floors, an inexpensive—and dirt-masking—alternative to refinishing a floor. To re-create them: Begin by painting the floor with a solid background. Once it's dry, dip a plastic fork into your secondary paint color and gently flick it onto the floor. You want random globs and clusters, not a uniform spread. Justine says, "Think small galaxies in the night sky, not Jackson Pollock."

07

Cot Coffee Table

Architects Robert Highsmith and Stefanie Brechbuehler, of Workstead, devised this clever new use for a World War II–era wooden army cot. To find one, search yard sales, eBay, and antiques stores—Robert found theirs in Maine for $15.

You need:

- Cot
- Drill
- Four wood struts to run the width of the cot (Workstead's were made from widely available ¾-inch-by-1½-inch square poplar trim)
- Six wooden pegs
- Hardwood plank (the one shown here is laminated pine)

STEP 1: Remove the existing canvas and strip out the staples (or leave them as a hint of the cot's past).

STEP 2: Drill six holes into the diagonal legs, at the desired height for the struts to support the top. Cut the struts to your desired length (about the width of the cot itself) and drill holes in each to match the location of the six holes. Secure the struts in place with the wooden pegs; use two in the center for support.

STEP 3: Cut the hardwood plank to the desired length.

STEP 4: Place the plank on top of the struts; secure if desired (Workstead's fits securely enough to just rest on top).

08

Hanging Planter and Utensils Rack

Created by architect Jen Turner (after a design by Vincent Vandenbrouck), this suspended shelf holds pots that can be filled with plants, kitchen things, or whatever you like. It hangs from a hook in the ceiling, and works equally well in a window or against a wall.

You need:

- One 48-inch-long-by-½-inch-wide-by-2-inch-deep poplar board cut into four pieces, each 9¾ inches long (you'll have leftover wood). You can usually get a hardware store employee to do the trimming for you.

- Two 48-inch-long, 1-inch-diameter wood dowels, cut into four pieces, each 19 inches long (you'll have leftover wood)

- Wood stain or paint (Jen used Cabot's solid wood stain in Dark Gray mixed with a little water to thin it)

- Drill

- Twelve stainless-steel eye hooks with ¼-inch-diameter eyes

- Approximately 20 feet of wire rope (Jen used McMaster-Carr's ¹⁄₁₆-inch vinyl-coated wire rope in red)

- Twelve zinc-plated copper compression sleeves for ¹⁄₈-inch wire (these secure the wire in place and are available from hardware stores)

- Vise and pliers or compression tool

- Six flowerpots, buckets, or other containers (shown here, 4¾-inch-diameter Mandel and Socker pots from Ikea)

STEP 1: Paint or stain the wooden pieces.

STEP 2: Drill two 1-inch-diameter holes in each slat spaced to hold your containers in place and approximately 1½ inches from the edge. Be sure to measure the diameter of each type of container.

STEP 3: Drill pilot holes for the eye hooks, locating them ¾ inch from the ends of each slat, and screw in hooks. The planter's top tier requires hooks on top and bottom; the bottom tier requires hooks only on the top.

STEP 4: Measure the desired length of top-tier wire from your ceiling. Attach one end of wire to an eye hook with a loop and a compression sleeve. Crimp the sleeve using the vise and pliers or the compression tool. Attach the other end of the wire to the second hook on the same slat, so that suspended they form a V.

STEP 5: For the lower tier, attach one end of desired length of wire to an eye hook and loop the other end to the corresponding hook on the upper tier. Do the same for the remaining hooks so that the tiers are parallel. The ones shown here are each 18 inches long.

STEP 6: Slide the dowels into place.

STEP 7: Hang the planter from the hooks anchored in your ceiling. Insert the containers and fill as desired.

09

Bright Baroque Mirror

To upgrade her children's bathroom, Catherine Dann grabbed a can of spray paint and recast a thrift-store mirror from Liberace's living room to Pee-wee's Playhouse. She used painter's tape to protect the mirror, and before hanging it, applied tape to the mirror's back to keep the orange edges from rubbing off on the wall. Similarly, she used a band of duct tape to give a soap dispenser some punch.

10

Spray-Painted Dresser Knobs

Upgrading a bureau can be as simple as painting the knobs—as evidenced by this plain Ikea dresser. To transform it, Sarah Lonsdale unscrewed the existing pulls, put them in a cardboard box, took them outside, and spray-painted them in one go.

PART 3

Where's the Stuff?

A close-up look at inspired solutions for coping
with modern clutter. In addition to attentive
editing—call it curating your museum—it all
boils down to this: you either display it or stow it.
Here, brilliant examples of both approaches.

01

Use Old Office Equipment as Kitchen Drawers

A tall, narrow set of metal drawers can have a second life as a kitchen repository, especially in a modern setting. Celebrated British chef, photographer, and shopkeeper Alastair Hendy finds his make a great utensil filing system for everything from knives to screwdrivers to skewers. And he keeps cream-colored ceramics in a vintage industrial cart.

02

Keep Batteries in Wooden Cutlery Trays

A wooden silverware divider is put to smart use organizing batteries and lightbulbs by size in Amanda Pays and Corbin Bernsen's well-equipped laundry room.

03

Sneak in Pocket Closets

Architects and designers like to walk around houses knocking on walls. They're looking for hidden treasure: a hollow space where shelves or a closet could be slipped in. In Francesca Connolly's dining room, two such pocket chambers contain all manner of essentials, from the blender to the family printer and telephone.

04

Hang Kitchen Supplies

Master of improvised kitchen solutions Alastair
Hendy uses lighting conduit to suspend notes and
recipes from clips and a scrub brush on a hook.

05

Store Everyday Cutlery in Tin Cans

When drawer space is at a minimum, consider keeping flatware in open receptacles. We're enamored of Rebecca Scott and Jerome Ranawake's use of ribbed tin cans with the labels peeled off.

06

Use Identical Clear Glass Jars for Storing Staples

Picture the grains, flours, and other essentials shown here in the packaging they came in and you'll instantly understand the advantages of decanting. Arranging kitchen goods in same-sized clear glass jars, as Michaela Scherrer does, is visually compelling, and allows you to see what you've got. We especially like the receptacles made by Weck (see "The Remodelista 100," page 333).

07

Stow the Microwave in a Cupboard

Aside from being space hogs, microwaves are no fun to look at. Architect Sheila Narusawa has an efficient solution: she hides hers (along with the toaster) in a kitchen cupboard with sliding drawers that she outfitted with electrical outlets.

08

Put a Kitchen Collection on Prominent Display

Café au lait bowls, gathered by a couple since their Paris honeymoon, are lined up on built-in shelves designed by Marco Pasanella and Rebecca Robertson. The display adds a whimsical element to an otherwise all-white kitchen, but the bowls themselves aren't treated as museum pieces: they're used daily and put in the dishwasher.

09

Turn a Hallway into an Instant Mudroom

For an organized entry, all you need are hardware-store metal hooks mounted under a wooden hat shelf, and metal trays for stowing shoes—as demonstrated by architect Sheila Narusawa. Galvanized-steel boot trays are available through garden-supply catalogs and Amazon.com.

Where's the Stuff?

Design Ideas

10

Hide Your Washing Machine

There are many ways to keep washing machines out of sight, most commonly by relegating them to the basement. But how much handier to have them close by— whether tucked into a curtained-off closet, fronted by a retractable door, or cordoned behind a sliding wood panel (as shown here in the kitchen at Dosa 818).

11

Create a Partition with Curtains

In lieu of walls, dramatic floor-to-ceiling curtains in Scott Newkirk's house keep a messy home office and kitchen out of sight. Made of inexpensive burlap edged on top with grommets, the curtains are suspended on standard-issue hospital tracks.

12

High to Low—Stack, Roll, and Tie It On

All rolls of toilet paper look much the same, but there are countless ways to present them. Here are a few of our favorites. Corinne Gilbert's homemade solution makes use of a painted wooden knob and a loop of ribbon. Opposite, clockwise from top left: A spare roll holder from classic Danish company D Line; Urban Archaeology's polished chrome Yale Club design, the Rolls-Royce of its kind; mod geometrics on a laundry room shelf; a woven basket with multi-roll capacity; a lawyer's bookcase as toiletry cabinet; and a Brancusi-esque tower of TP.

The Remodelista 100

Presenting our all-time favorite everyday objects: from wastebaskets to teakettles, these humble essentials are enduring, life-enhancing, and often extremely affordable.

With nutshell histories by Megan Wilson, owner of AncientIndustries.com.

01 Vipp Pedal Bin

A Danish modernist classic that has been in production since 1939, Vipp was created as a one-off by twenty-four-year-old Holger Nielsen for his wife Marie's beauty salon in Copenhagen. The lidded, powder-coated steel bin had an air of medicinal chic about it, which caught the eye of many of Marie's customers who happened to be married to dentists and doctors. The orders poured in, and Nielsen was in business. "Good design never goes out of fashion," he said, and after his death, his daughter, Jette, increased Vipp's global popularity with the help of the Conran Shop. Today Vipp is in the permanent collection at the Museum of Modern Art.

WHY IT WORKS: Almost too attractive to be called a garbage can
WHERE TO GET IT: vipp.com, allmodern.com

02 Duralex Gigogne Tumbler

We barely need to say that these are made in France, so closely are they associated with café au lait, beret-wearing schoolchildren, baguettes, and *vin de table.* Duralex emerged during World War II and developed molded, tempered glass at its factory in Orléans. Fired with extreme heat followed by a rapid cooling system, this glass is virtually unbreakable, which has made it indispensable in cafés and school lunchrooms. The Gigogne ("nesting," in French) was introduced in 1946 and is in the permanent collection of the Musée des Arts Decoratifs in Paris.

WHY IT WORKS: Inimitably French and indestructible
WHERE TO GET IT: duralexusa.com

03 Swedish Brush and Dustpan

Paired by Kiosk in New York, this dustpan and brush come from two small manufacturers in Sweden. The powder-coated steel pan is a traditional design from a factory in Gnosjö. The horsehair-and-beech brush is made by hand at Iris Hantverk, a foundation in Stockholm that has provided work for the visually impaired since the late nineteenth century. In both, there is an absence of synthetic materials, which is what usually confines these cleaning items to the back of the cupboard.

WHY IT WORKS: Attractive and durable
WHERE TO GET IT: kioskkiosk.com

04 Oil and Vinegar Cruet

Long before British and American housewives were alerted to the joys of Mediterranean cooking, the Spanish were buying olive oil by the gallon and using it liberally in the kitchen. In 1961 Catalan industrial designer Rafael Marquina created a revolutionary oil cruet that was handier than wielding a large can and, more important, did not drip. Aside from its functionality, there is something pleasingly pharmaceutical about the clink of the glass as one replaces the slender spout after refilling the cruet. Useful also for vinegar or dishwashing soap.

WHY IT WORKS: Nondrip and easy to pour
WHERE TO GET IT: foodiekitchen.com

05 Original BTC Hector Light

A relatively young company that looks to the past, Original BTC was founded by Peter Bowles in 1990. An early advocate of industrial chic, he takes his inspiration from a variety of unexpected sources, ranging from the searchlight on an antique toy truck to the cord snipped from the family iron. The Hector Wall Light was introduced in 1992 and uses the company's trademark mix of materials like steel, bone china, and braided cotton-covered cording.

WHY IT WORKS: Modern yet traditional
WHERE TO GET IT: shophorne.com

06 General's Cedar Pointe Pencils

There is something particularly American about an old-fashioned wooden pencil, especially when it is made of sustainable California incense cedar, which gives off a faint aroma of the forest. General Pencil was begun by a German immigrant named Edward Weissenborn, who had a hand in constructing the Civil War battleship USS *Monitor* before founding his factory in New Jersey in 1889 with his son. Six generations of Weissenborns later, the pencils are still in demand by artists, writers, and grocery-list makers.

WHY THEY WORK: Made of sustainable wood
WHERE TO GET THEM: generalpencil.com

07 Korbo Wire Basket

In 1922 it was thought prudent to make baskets for fishermen and farmers that would not rust or deteriorate in the salt air and wind of Sweden. Korbo, which means "basket" in Swedish, is as simple in structure as it is in name: using a single length of steel wire, the baskets are woven without welding, which makes them virtually indestructible. Fortunately for us the tradition continues, and the Korbo is just as useful for holding laundry, logs, and magazines as it is for holding fish and potatoes.

WHY IT WORKS: Elegant, indestructible, and rustproof
WHERE TO GET IT: dwr.com, canoe.net

08 Tivoli Audio Model One Radio

With a frugal Yankee design reminiscent of the Kennedy era, this powerful sound in a wooden box can trace its roots to midcentury Cambridge, Massachusetts. Henry Kloss, an MIT dropout who added the *K* to KLH Audio in 1957, was responsible for the first acoustic suspension loudspeaker small enough to fit on a bookshelf. In a highly stylized era, he eschewed current design trends in favor of efficiency and longevity, and in 1960 he came up with the KLH Model Eight FM table radio. More like a working prototype in its utilitarian design, the Model Eight consisted of a wooden frame surrounding a white face, three black knobs, and a radio dial. In 2001 Kloss emerged from a brief retirement to give us the Model One, a direct nod to the Model Eight, but with two knobs instead of three. That's progress.

WHY IT WORKS: Discreet design, big sound
WHERE TO GET IT: tivoliaudio.com

09 Butterfly Chair

Popularly associated with midcentury modernist lounging, the Butterfly began life as a wood-framed folding chair used during the Crimean and Boer wars and was patented by the British in 1877. Fifty years later, three Argentine architects replaced the wood with a single length of steel and exhibited the chair at a furniture fair in Buenos Aires. It caught the eye of MoMA's industrial design curator, Edgar Kaufmann Jr., who bought one for the museum and one for his parents' new country house, Fallingwater (designed by Frank Lloyd Wright). Knoll acquired the U.S. production rights in 1947, and about 5 million chairs were sold during the 1950s alone. Today the chair is faithfully reproduced by Circa 50 in Vermont.

WHY IT WORKS: Casual, affordable, and looks good anywhere
WHERE TO GET IT: circa50.com, steelecanvas.com

10 Heath Ceramics Coupe Line

Economy was central to Edith Heath's vision. Economy of line became her trademark, and economy of materials was ingrained from helping to raise six siblings during the Depression. In the mid-1940s Edith's husband, Brian, built a kiln and converted a tread-pedaled sewing machine into a potter's wheel, and Edith was able to put into practice her vision of "simple, good things for good people." Using local clay sourced from Sacramento, California, she created her own distinctive glazing and fired the clay at energy-efficient temperatures. Her designs were functional with a modernist elegance; when she opened her factory in Sausalito in 1948, she introduced the Coupe line. A decidedly understated dinner collection, it was embraced by Frank Lloyd Wright for use in several architectural projects and was later championed by Alice Waters at Chez Panisse when the Heath factory was revived at the turn of the twenty-first century.

WHY IT WORKS: Conscientious everyday chic
WHERE TO GET IT: heathceramics.com

11 Anglepoise Type75 Lamp

A lamp that maintains great poise at rakish angles, the Anglepoise was created by automotive engineer George Carwardine in his garage in Bath, England. The arm-like joints and spring tension enabled the lamp to cast light at specific angles, and it was first popular with doctors and dentists before being adapted for the home. In 2004 Kenneth Grange, famous for the Kenwood Mixer, the Parker Pen, the black cab, and other British icons, created the more streamlined Anglepoise Type75, which soon became a classic in its own right.

WHY IT WORKS: Practical for any room
WHERE TO GET IT: lumens.com, anglepoise.com

12 Shaker Pegs

With a design aesthetic as finely tuned as that of the Bauhaus, the Shakers were the greatest industrial designers never to have gone to art school. Otherwise known as the United Society of Believers in Christ's Second Appearing, the Shakers believed that making things well was an act of prayer. They established their self-sustaining villages from Maine to Kentucky toward the end of the eighteenth century and set about stripping away embellishment at a time when too much embellishment was still not enough. Although the movement has since died out, the furniture is still made by hand, and the useful and affordable Shaker peg lives on.

WHY THEY WORK: Timeless, understated order
WHERE TO GET THEM: shakerworkshops.com

13 Staub Cooking Pots

At a family-owned cookware shop in Alsace, the founder's grandson, Francis Staub, decided to try his hand at designing pots himself. His first *coquette,* or Dutch oven, was designed in 1974, and with the acquisition of a local cast-iron factory, Staub was in business. What sets Staub products apart from other enamel-coated cast-iron wares on the market is their clean, industrial design and unapologetically masculine colors. Coated with double-glazed enamel, the pots are virtually indestructible. Choose a Staub with care, because it will be a friend for life.

WHY THEY WORK: Heat efficiency in sober colors
WHERE TO GET THEM: staubusa.com

14 Bialetti Moka Express Coffeemaker

Gazing into a washing machine one day, Alfonso Bialetti realized that the pressure action of the hot water rising through a funnel to flood the drum of the machine could be applied to coffee making. In 1933 the Moka Express was born, and for several years, Alfonso sold it at the local market in Piedmont, Italy. Because good-quality coffee had until then been obtainable only with the aid of an industrial-sized espresso machine, the Moka Express soon caught on, and today nine out of ten households in Italy have one. The *l'omino coi baffi,* or "mustachioed little man," is a caricature trademark of Alfonso's son, Renato, who took over the company in 1946.

WHY IT WORKS: Café-quality coffee at home
WHERE TO GET IT: bialettishop.com, momastore.org

15 Weber Grill

One of the most iconic symbols of American summertime, the Weber grill was developed by a welder in 1952 at the Weber Brothers Metal Works. Fed up with the caveman approach to grilling meat, George Stephen realized when joining the two halves of a metal buoy together that he could create an enclosed and therefore more efficient grill. He poked some holes in the side for ventilation and took "George's Barbecue Kettle" on the road to sell to hardware stores across the country. The grills were so popular that George bought the Weber factory.

WHY IT WORKS: Enclosed grilling with classic style
WHERE TO GET IT: homedepot.com, acehardware.com

16 Miele Vacuum Cleaner

Founded in Germany in 1899 by Carl Miele and Reinhard Zinkann, Miele has manufactured everything from butter churners to cars and bicycles to handcarts. But it wasn't until 1931 that the company had a go at vacuum cleaners. Miele's motto is *Immer Besser* (Forever Better), and Miele has applied this motto to washing machines, refrigerators, dishwashers, and ovens, along with its peerless vacuum cleaner. With its power, efficiency, and sleek design, the Miele makes vacuuming (almost) fun.

WHY IT WORKS: Quiet and efficient
WHERE TO GET IT: gracioushome.com, bedbathandbeyond.com

17 French Enamel House Numbers

Around the time that Baron Haussmann was reorganizing Paris, street signs and house numbers were being reconsidered, too. With a resilient surface of ground glass, the porcelain enamel sign could withstand the various weather conditions of this northern city, as well as the vigor of city life. Enamel signs were until then made only in black and white. We don't know who decided to add chromium dioxide as a color pigment, but the result was a form of ultramarine easily spotted across a wide boulevard. The blue *vêtements de travail,* or "French work uniform," followed suit, and blue became the color of efficiency in France.

WHY THEY WORK: Functional French design at its best
WHERE TO GET THEM: ramsign.com

18 Iittala Lempi Wineglass

Iittala takes its name from the area in Finland where this glass factory began in 1881. Swedish glassblowers were imported to Iittala because of a lack of skill in Finland; and although there is no lack of Finnish designers today, Swedish talent is still being imported. Mindful of modern restricted kitchens, the Swedish designer Matti Klenell designed these easily stackable glasses. The short, sturdy stems add an informality that makes the glasses welcome on the breakfast table, but the elegant shape ensures that they have a place at the dinner table, too.

WHY IT WORKS: Stackable glasses for breakfast or dinner
WHERE TO GET IT: fjorn.com

19 Corin Mellor Birch Plywood Tray

Like his father, David, the celebrated industrial designer Corin Mellor grew up in the silversmith capital of Sheffield, England. Corin trained in London as a product designer and is now the creative director of his father's company. In 2007 he introduced a range of glass, kitchen knives, and wood products for David Mellor. His birch plywood tray, with its rounded corners and hand-sized openings at each end, begs to be displayed as a permanent fixture—on the liquor cabinet, for instance—rather than hidden away in the cupboard.

WHY IT WORKS: A tray that can be displayed
WHERE TO GET IT: davidmellordesign.com

20 Eena Work Apron

When the Chinook peoples populated Portland, Oregon, the word *eena* meant "the beaver who builds the best house." We may not know what the word for the less-industrious beaver was, but the people at the Beckel Canvas Products company decided that Eena was a good trademark for their Portland-based company. Keeping things really local, their friends around the corner at Canoe asked them to make some products for their shop, and this simple and practical black apron was born.

WHY IT WORKS: A unisex apron that hides stains
WHERE TO GET IT: canoeonline.net

21 Växbo Lin Dishcloth

Woven in a beautiful old wooden mill owned by a fantastically attractive couple, Hanna and Jacob Bruce, in the impossibly bucolic town of Hälsingland, these Swedish dishcloths deserve their hallowed status. At Växbo the flax is spun and woven using traditional methods that ensure that the resulting linen is highly absorbent as well as quick-drying. With their prettily exposed selvedge, not only are the cloths attractive, they also love to be washed, and only improve with age. And so we must ask: what are you still doing with that smelly old synthetic sponge?

WHY IT WORKS: Loves to clean and be cleaned
WHERE TO GET IT: ingebretsens.com

22 IBM Clock

The IBM clock has been quietly marking time in American schoolrooms, offices, and factories for almost a hundred years. This midcentury example with the pre–Paul Rand logo was designed by unknown sources, but its understated and ubiquitous presence left an indelible impression on a generation of bored or harried workers across the land. Reproduced by Schoolhouse Electric, it's assembled in Oregon from clock pieces that are made in the United States.

WHY IT WORKS: Timeless timepiece
WHERE TO GET IT: schoolhouseelectric.com

23 David Mellor Pride Cutlery

"Well-designed equipment can improve your life" was the operating principle of David Mellor, a designer, manufacturer, and retailer. Mellor was born in Sheffield, England, a city associated with cutlery since medieval times, so it's easy to believe that his destiny was fixed at birth. After attending the Royal College of Art during the 1951 Festival of Britain, he could not help being swept up by the pride in postwar British design. Mellor designed his first six-piece cutlery set while still at college and named it Pride. Put into production in 1953, the sleek and enduringly elegant flatware with resin handle options has been in continuous production in Sheffield ever since.

WHY IT WORKS: At once casual and dressy
WHERE TO GET IT: heathceramics.com, davidmellordesign.com

24 U.S. Mailbox

Back when the fire and police departments were made up of rivaling factions, U.S. Mail was an organization in similar disarray. Rural routes were dotted with handmade mailboxes that did not necessarily fare well in snow, nor rain, nor sleet. In 1915 a standard mailbox was designed by postal engineer Roy Joroleman: it was essentially an oversize tin can with a latched door and a flat base for a post. Beyond the addition of the jaunty red flag, the classic mailbox has barely changed over the years, and it remains a symbol of domestic American life in all terrains and climates.

WHY IT WORKS: An American icon still made in America
WHERE TO GET IT: gibraltarmailboxes.com

25 Berea College Crafts Fireplace Broom

Kentucky's Berea College is an unusual place. Founded by an abolitionist in 1855, it was the first integrated, coeducational school in America. The college is one of only a handful to follow a work-study program that enables students to attend tuition-free while gaining skills in pottery, weaving, cabinetry, and broom making. Profits from these handcrafted products support the students. The designs are traditional Appalachian, and this influence is most evident in the brooms, which follow the same methods that were in use before the Civil War. The fireplace broom, rolled by hand from black straw, is an example of early American practicality that is increasingly difficult to find.

WHY IT WORKS: Made of hard-wearing, nonmelting straw
WHERE TO GET IT: bereacollegecrafts.com

26 Bürstenhaus Redecker Copper Cloth

Before abrasive chemicals were introduced into household cleaning, homemakers used natural ingredients, such as lemon juice and vinegar, to remove stains. And instead of synthetic sponges, there were dishcloths made of cotton or woven copper. Because copper is a soft metal, it gently but firmly lifts stubborn dirt from enamel, glass, and steel with the aid of water. The cloths are also useful for removing rust as well as for polishing chrome, making them indispensable in both the kitchen and the garage. They're manufactured by Redecker, a German brush company that knows a thing or two about cleaning with natural materials.

WHY IT WORKS: Chemical- and odor-free
WHERE TO GET IT: surlatable.com

27 Sori Yanagi Teakettle

A Japanese modernist most famous for his graceful 1956 Butterfly Stool, Sori Yanagi designed this brushed stainless-steel kettle forty years later. Taking inspiration from designers like Le Corbusier and Alvar Aalto, Yanagi also looked to everyday objects, like the baseball glove, that evolved over time. The reason half a million Japanese households buy a Sori Yanagi kettle every year is that its wider-than-normal base allows for a swifter boil, and the holes punched in the side of the lid allow the steam to escape sideways instead of up toward the handle. Enduring good looks may also have something to do with it.

WHY IT WORKS: Burn-free boiling experience
WHERE TO GET IT: brookfarmgeneralstore.com

28 Bonsai Scissors

Many centuries before the Shakers and the modernists, Japanese craftsmen were doing their bit for functional minimalism. Although they cannot claim to have invented the cross-blade scissor (the Romans got there first), they did develop this fluid shape, which accommodates the entire hand rather than just the forefinger and thumb. With a short, sharp blade, the scissors are associated with the trimming of bonsai trees, but they are indispensable in the garden and around the house as well. Made on the island of Tanegashima since the twelfth century, they are still being fashioned there today.

WHY THEY WORK: Twelfth-century ergonomics
WHERE TO GET THEM: bonsaioutlet.com, tortoisegeneralstore.com

29 Peterboro Picnic Basket

Peterboro Baskets, established 150 years ago in Peterborough, New Hampshire, is the oldest basket-weaving factory in the United States. Its wares are woven with flat strips of Appalachian ash gathered in New Hampshire, Maine, and Vermont. The picnic basket, which can be ordered with a bicycle attachment, is Wicked Witch of the West meets Thornton Wilder—a thoroughly American basket that is just right for carrying picnics and little dogs, too.

WHY IT WORKS: Useful for picnics, bicycles, and storage
WHERE TO GET IT: peterborobasket.com

30 Opinel Knife

Joseph Opinel was just nineteen when he designed his eponymous pocketknife in 1890. The son of a toolmaker, he grew up in the Savoie region of the French Alps, an area known for its axes and pruning knives. With a blade that tucks tidily into the wood handle, the knives proved understandably popular with Joseph's teenage friends. But Joseph was a clever businessman, too. He set up a shop by the train station, selling knives to rail workers, who spread the word throughout France. By 1897 there were eleven sizes of Opinel knife, and by the start of World War II, more than 20 million knives had been sold.

WHY IT WORKS: Sleek, sharp, and portable
WHERE TO GET IT: opinel-usa.com

31 Felicity Irons Rush Table Mat

Once the floor cover of choice in Elizabethan households, rush has fallen so far from popular fashion that only one company still harvests it in England. Felicity Irons (sister of Jeremy) and a few family members harvest up to two tons a day during the summer months from the rivers Ouse, Nene, and Ivel. As it dries, various colors reveal themselves: if the conditions are fair, the rush is bleached to a honey tone; if the weather is windy, the rush turns a vivid green hue. Equally at home in a castle or a cottage, rush matting is again finding a place for itself across the land.

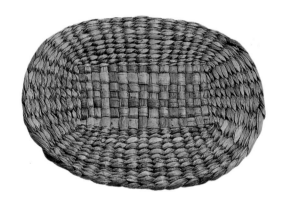

WHY IT WORKS: Ancient craft from a renewable source
WHERE TO GET IT: rushmatters.co.uk, davidmellordesign.com

32 Brown Betty Teapot

Of the myriad selection of teapots available, the Brown Betty has always distinguished herself above all others. She eschews fashion and the latest trends (including her greatest rival, bone china), never straying from her path toward a good cup of tea. Back before Josiah Wedgwood was born, a red clay was discovered near Stoke-on-Trent, England, that was especially admired for its ability to retain heat. During the Empire, when Britain was awash with tea, the rounded teapot evolved and Brown Betty found her place in polite society quicker than one could say "China or India?"

WHY IT WORKS: Short, stout, and heat-retaining
WHERE TO GET IT: englishteastore.com

33 Zangra Industrial Light

For such a diminutive country, Belgium has brought us bountiful gifts: Tintin, Audrey Hepburn, Luc Tuymans, Brussels sprouts, and the saxophone, to name a few. It's time to add one more—Zangra, a young company begun by architect-turned-manufacturer (and general procurer of cool stuff) Eve van Dyck. Out of a frustration with modern light fixtures, van Dyck had some antique light sockets copied by a porcelain factory. She kept some and sold the rest to her architect friends, who soon wanted more. Before long, she was producing a variety of light fixtures and other household goods. "Sell the things you like," says Eve, who, happily, has an eye for the hard-to-find and the irresistible.

WHY IT WORKS: Effortlessly chic
WHERE TO GET IT: zangra.com

34 Steele Canvas Hamper

From their unhemmed raw canvas to their handwrought stenciled logo, Steele's large, mobile hampers exude an aura of uncomplicated practicality. They're made by a family-run company that has been operating just north of Boston since 1921. And while intended for use on building sites and in the transportation and storage of dry goods, Steele hampers are today just as likely to be put to work in the laundry room, garage, or playroom.

WHY IT WORKS: Homely industrial design for home or industry
WHERE TO GET IT: steelecanvas.com

35 Chemex Coffeemaker

If this filter coffeemaker looks as if it strayed from a science lab, it might be because it was designed by a chemist. In 1941 Dr. Peter Schlumbohm, a German immigrant, created the first Chemex, using an Erlenmeyer flask and a glass laboratory funnel. The basic theory and shape have never changed—coffee purists can get quite scientific about its superiority over the coffee press. Within three years the Chemex was in the collection at the Museum of Modern Art, and in 1963 it was James Bond's coffeemaker of choice in the film *From Russia with Love*.

WHY IT WORKS: Controlled drip for a purer coffee
WHERE TO GET IT: chemexcoffeemaker.com

36 English Oak Doorstop

FSC, or Forest Stewardship Council, is an international and growing nonprofit. It was founded in 1992 by a band of rogue businessmen and environmentalists concerned about deforestation. They suggested that the world's forests be managed more responsibly; in short, they advocated replanting trees and keeping the woods alive. These FSC oak doorstops might have once stood in an ancient wood, but one can sleep at night knowing it has not since been flattened. Their cunning, cheese-like wedge ensures that they slide discreetly under a variety of door heights, proving very handy in a sudden gust of wind.

WHY IT WORKS: A useful and conscientious substitute for plastic
WHERE TO GET IT: ancientindustries.com

37 Utensil Family by Jasper Morrison

This brushed-steel utensil set possesses such a sophisticated simplicity, it runs the risk of disappearing among the clutter of the kitchen—except it doesn't, because it's always orderly. The design ethos of Jasper Morrison, born in London in 1959, can be summed up in his rack of tools: they evoke a familiarity that in turn creates a feeling of trust. And that's not a bad feeling in the kitchen.

WHY IT WORKS: Five cooking essentials in a row
WHERE TO GET IT: allmodern.com

38 Waiter's Friend Corkscrew

Among the many corkscrews available, from the elaborate to the rudimentary, we always return to this neat folding contraption that is the most basic and reliable. Patented in Germany in 1882, Karl F. A. Wienke's original design has remained unaltered. With its lever, screw, and knife (for removing foil), the contraption folds neatly and safely into the pocket. Waiters the world over swear by it.

WHY IT WORKS: Compact and efficient
WHERE TO GET IT: brookfarmgeneralstore.com

39 Ferro & Fuoco Fireplace Tools

Translated as Iron and Fire, these Italian fireplace tools were designed by Marco Ferreri in 2000. Walking through an ancient Italian village, Ferreri discovered that the locals were forging gardening tools by hand out of disused railroad tracks. Although a very contemporary furniture designer by nature, he was inspired to design a fire poker, tongs, and an ash shovel to be made in the same village by the same methods. Each tool is triple-coated with a black powder finish for extra durability.

WHY THEY WORK: Ancient yet modern recycled hearth accessories
WHERE TO GET THEM: loftmodern.com

40 Riess Aromapot

Since 1550 iron pans and kettles have been made in the water-powered town of Ybbsitz, Austria. At the turn of the nineteenth century, Johann Riess began his company, and eventually iron production turned to steel and thence to enamel-covered steel. In recent years, noted designers have been invited to work at the Riess factory, including Dottings, a Vienna company that was commissioned to create a line of enamel pots that stack easily for the space-challenged kitchen. The lid performs a double function: when turned upside down, it becomes a trivet.

WHY IT WORKS: Sleek and stackable
WHERE TO GET IT: twentytwentyone.com, objectsofuse.com

41 Painters' Drop Cloth

To the DIY enthusiast, as well as the cash-strapped, the painter's drop cloth is unbeatable in terms of quality, price, and versatility. Huge and hemmed, the raw, unbleached cotton sheet can be used for sewing curtains and shades, painting floor cloths, creating ad hoc slipcovers, and, in the spirit of Maria von Trapp, fashioning very chic children's clothes. It also makes the perfect tablecloth.

WHY IT WORKS: The mother of all fabrics
WHERE TO GET IT: homedepot.com and hardware stores nationwide

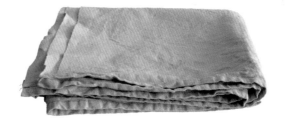

42 Noguchi Akari Lamp

"Everything is sculpture," said Isamu Noguchi, and his Akari light is a very good example of this belief. Born in the United States to a Japanese father and an American mother, he was a distinguished sculptor and set designer before producing the iconic Noguchi table for Herbert Miller in 1947. When traveling in Japan in 1951, he was asked to create a paper lamp for export to help revitalize the paper manufacturing industry there. The Akari lamp, Noguchi's modernist response to lanterns used by night fishermen in Japan, represented the form stripped down to its bones, all color and extraneous decorative detail discarded. Because the lamps were made of little more than rice paper and wire, they were inexpensive to produce and affordable. Ozeki & Co. has been manufacturing them by hand since 1951—and continues to do so, packing the lamps flat for easy shipping.

WHY IT WORKS: A sculptural light with a soft glow
WHERE TO GET IT: noguchi.org

43 Emile Henry Urban Pitcher

While others were planting vines in the soil of Burgundy, Emile Henry was using the soil for clay. The mineral-rich limestone clay of this terroir proved to be an excellent conductor and retainer of heat when fired into pots. Emile Henry cookware can be easily transferred from hot to cold temperatures without cracking of clay or crazing of glaze. The 1-quart pitcher is tall and thin and can be fit into the door of a refrigerator.

WHY IT WORKS: Traditional with a modern profile
WHERE TO GET IT: emilehenryusa.com

44 Lodge Cast-Iron Skillet

Founded in the Appalachian mountains of Kentucky, Joseph Lodge's company is the oldest family-run iron foundry in America. Iron skillets do not wear out, which makes them perhaps the most economical investment for the kitchen. Yes, they do need to be seasoned with vegetable oil in a hot oven periodically, and no, your well-meaning houseguest should not wash the pan with soap, but this care only adds to the ritual of cooking with cast iron. Slow to heat but consistent when hot, Lodge's multipurpose skillet should always be kept within easy reach.

WHY IT WORKS: The workhorse of the stove
WHERE TO GET IT: lodgemfg.com

45 Milton Brook Mortar and Pestle

Made in Stoke-on-Trent, England, using vitrified porcelain, both mortar and pestle are completely nonabsorbent—essential when mixing spices and adopted by the pharmaceutical industry for this reason as well. The unvarnished beech-wood handle provides a good nonslip grip, too.

WHY IT WORKS: Understated, nonabsorbent functionality
WHERE TO GET IT: canoeonline.net

46 Dover Parkersburg 2.25-Gallon Tub

Dover Parkersburg has been in the utilitarian product business since 1833. Based in Virginia, the company provides a range of buckets, cans, and tubs for use in the garden or on the farm. What sets these humble vessels apart is that they are made of steel that has been "hot-dipped" in molten zinc to achieve a far less corrosive coating. The galvanized finish produces a bright prismatic shine that softens to matte as it ages. The 2.25-gallon tub is 15 inches long and multitasks as a planter, an ice bucket, or a storage container.

WHY IT WORKS: Rustproof steel for outdoors and in
WHERE TO GET IT: mainstsupply.com

47 Schoolhouse Electric Alabax Pendant Light

This pendant is named after the Parker & Seymour Alabax lamps that were so popular in American bathrooms and hospitals between the wars. Schoolhouse Electric has revived the style, with porcelain made in Portland, Oregon.

WHY IT WORKS: Clinical-chic ceiling porcelain
WHERE TO GET IT: schoolhouseelectric.com

48 Toilet Brush and Bucket

Before London emporium Labour and Wait was bold enough to look cleaning utensils in the eye, brushes and buckets had long been banned to the back of the closet, punished for being born ugly and destined for a short life. Labour and Wait discovered that somewhere abroad, household brushes were still being made by hand out of long-lasting wood and bristle. Out of the broom cupboard came the dustpan and brush, the broom and the feather duster, and out from that dark corner came the toilet brush. It was also Labour and Wait's genius idea to house the toilet brush in a galvanized gardening pot, an original pairing that is proud to take its place in the open.

WHY IT WORKS: A necessity worthy of display
WHERE TO GET IT: labourandwait.co.uk

49 Fort Standard Stone Trivet

Take the Brooklyn-bound Ikea ferry from Wall Street, and the first point of Red Hook that swings into view is an impressive redbrick Civil War warehouse abutting the water. At this point you wish you could ask the skipper to pull up to the wharf and allow you to disembark. Among the many creative tenants within are Fort Standard, a bewhiskered duo who work with metal and stone and wood, creating contemporary shapes from ancient materials. Their marble trivets are essentially modern, and yet the hexagonal cut of the marble suggests that they might have looked at home in Renaissance Italy.

WHY IT WORKS: An understated mix of ancient and modern
WHERE TO GET IT: thefutureperfect.com

50 Caravaggio P2 Pendant Light

"Design should never receive greater focus than the light itself," says Cecilie Manz, who is equally comfortable working with wood, steel, linen, and glass. Designed in 2005, the Caravaggio pendant light was named for the artist who was so adept at conveying the contrast of light and chiaroscuro in his painting. It comes in black and white only and embraces a feminine form with masculine technology. Inspired by twentieth-century factory lighting, the Caravaggio is made of powder-coated steel and has a red cord and an opening at the top that allows for ambient upward light.

WHY IT WORKS: A celebration of light, dark, and shadow
WHERE TO GET IT: ylighting.com, danishdesignstore.com

51 Muuto Toss Around Salad Servers

Designed for Muuto in Copenhagen by design group KiBiSi, these white beech-wood salad servers, in the words of the designers, "unify form, function, and craftsmanship."

WHY THEY WORK: Minimalism for the salad bowl
WHERE TO GET THEM: finnishdesignshop.com

52 Coyuchi Organic Cotton Bed Linen

The collective conscience of "Coyuchis," or the people who work at this Northern California company, is so clean that when questioned by the jury of the buying public, they always have the answer at the ready. Why do you produce in India? "Because India has one of the greatest textiles industries in the world." Why don't you cut and sew in the United States? "Because all of the large cut-and-sew facilities have closed down." What does *coyuchi* mean? "*Coyuchi* is a word used in southern Mexico for naturally colored brown cotton." Why buy Coyuchi? "As the first company to bring organic cotton to the United States, we can be counted on to keep your family safe from harmful chemicals."

WHY IT WORKS: Conscientious cotton
WHERE TO GET IT: coyuchi.com

53 Sheila Maid Clothes Airer

Who is Sheila? Was she a maid? And was it on a particularly rainy day a century ago in England that she was found fiddling with ropes, pulleys, and pine slats to create this ingenious clothes dryer? Whatever the origins, we can be certain of one thing: the Sheila Maid is an energy-efficient and aesthetically pleasing way to dry laundry, hoisted to the rafters, where the warm air gathers, then lowered for accessibility.

WHY IT WORKS: Space- and energy-saving
WHERE TO GET IT: ancientindustries.com

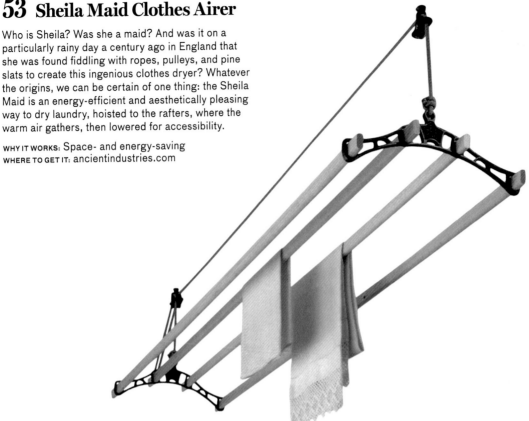

54 Holmegaard Minima Carafe

Holmegaard, founded in 1825 by a recently bereaved Danish countess, is a factory that still holds to Henriette Danneskiold-Samsøe's quest for glass with "heart and soul and integrity." The Minima collection, launched in 2007, is a perfect example of this ethos, mixing elegant form with today's need for space-saving function. Designed by Cecilie Manz, the carafe is as at home in the fridge, filled with milk or juice (where it is careful not to hog any space), as it is on the dinner table filled with wine. And to help retain the flavor of its contents, the carafe has a discreet plastic lid.

WHY IT WORKS: Tall, slim, elegant, and useful
WHERE TO GET IT: fjorn.com

55 Iittala Teema Dinnerware

Designed in 1952 by leading Finnish designer Kaj Franck, Teema is the embodiment of Franck's minimalist design ethos. The dinnerware set, which includes platters and lidded casserole dishes, is inspired by the simple forms of the circle, square, and rectangle. Pared down until there is nothing left to pare, Teema dinnerware provides the perfect backdrop for the food itself.

WHY IT WORKS: Naked elegance at the dining table
WHERE TO GET IT: fjorn.com, allmodern.com

56 Heath Ceramics Neutra House Numbers

Neutraface has all the sleek and elegant qualities of a font designed during the 1930s, and it practically shouts California: Hollywood, orange crates, modernism, and glass houses. Richard Neutra, designer of many glass houses, is the inspiration for Neutraface. It was created in 2002 by Christian Schwartz, who worked with Neutra's son to create a font that encapsulated the principles of the man. House Industries released Neutraface to instant acclaim and, with Heath Ceramics, decided to apply the architecture-inspired font to architecture.

WHY THEY WORK: California modernism distilled in a number
WHERE TO GET THEM: heathceramics.com

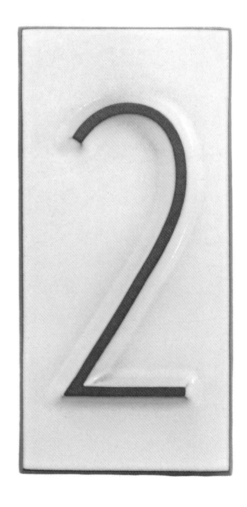

57 John Boos Cutting Board

Founded in 1897 in Effingham, Illinois, John Boos is one of the earliest butcher-block companies in America. Thanks to the edge-grain construction of its designs, the knife cuts into the grain, rather than across it, thus preserving the blade and increasing the life of the board. John Boos chopping boards are made of maple, a hardwood known for its durability.

WHY IT WORKS: An understated chopping board that cares about your blade
WHERE TO GET IT: surlatable.com

58 Otto Fan

Pin-drop-quiet with an industrial-strength breeze, this bamboo-clad fan is Swiss efficiency at its best. Designed by Carlo Borer, an extremely productive designer who is equally at home with electric kettles, deck chairs, and mailboxes, the Otto fan will discreetly cool a room from tabletop or floor.

WHY IT WORKS: Strong and silent with a cool presence
WHERE TO GET IT: stadlerformusa.com

59 Peugeot Pepper Mill

Before the Peugeot car and the Peugeot bicycle, there was the Peugeot pepper mill. Having converted a grain mill in the French Alps into a steel mill, the Peugeot family set about making umbrella frames, crinoline petticoat rods, and other essential household items. Interested in the technical side of things, they created a wooden pepper mill with a steel mechanism that cracks the peppercorn and then grinds it in a double spiral of teeth. Its strong-jawed interior was the inspiration for the Peugeot lion.

WHY IT WORKS: Race-car-style grinding
WHERE TO GET IT: surlatable.com, oldfaithfulshop.com

60 Alvar Aalto Model 60 Stacking Stool

Alvar Aalto is largely responsible for making Finland the great modernist outpost. He was born in 1898 and got started early, opening his first architectural practice at twenty-five and later collaborating with his wife, the influential architect and designer Aino Aalto. Together they embraced the design ethic of *Gesamtkunstwerk,* or "total work of art." Their way to design a building was to attend to all the furnishings, glass, and lighting as well as the architecture. Alvar Aalto was a great fan of wood—it's warm to the touch and pliable. He especially loved birch, and through experimentation was able to make it bend. The L-shaped legs found on these versatile stools create a seamless-looking structure, and are especially pretty when stacked.

WHY IT WORKS: The stacking stool that doubles as a table
WHERE TO GET IT: hivemodern.com

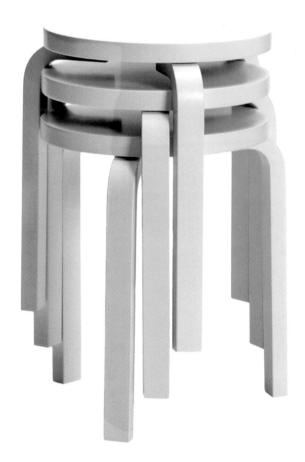

61 Tolomeo Clip Lamp

The Tolomeo lamp was designed in Milan by Michele de Lucchi, a member of the renegade Memphis Group, which took the design world by storm in the early 1980s. The Tolomeo is Memphis all grown up; it is all about streamlined efficiency, discreetly lighting a room without ever calling attention to itself. Made of matte anodized aluminum, the shade is small yet powerful and can be fully rotated and tilted with the aid of a tiny heat-repellent steel rod. The light, which is available in floor, wall, and tabletop models, has, like Memphis, been a huge success in spite of itself, and is especially useful in kitchens and offices.

WHY IT WORKS: Discreet elegance and efficiency
WHERE TO GET IT: dwr.com

62 Beeswax Candles

Beeswax, an ingenious by-product of the female honeybee, has been used over the years not only for building beehives but for casting metal, printing textiles, polishing wood, sealing letters, and, of course, making candles. Though the world is filled with paraffin-based candles, our vote for best dinner light goes to the slow-burning beeswax taper, thanks to its pollen-infused color and subtle honey scent.

WHY THEY WORK: Sweet-smelling natural candlelight
WHERE TO GET THEM: kaufmann-mercantile.com, beeswaxcandleworks.com

63 Steel Wastebasket

The midcentury schoolroom and office metal can makes a comeback. Fabricated in the United States of stamped steel with a rolled edge, it brings back memories of mimeographed homework sheets and green-uniformed janitors.

WHY IT WORKS: Waste efficiency in an iconic package
WHERE TO GET IT: schoolhouseelectric.com

64 Flex-i-File

Patented in 1941 by Luther W. Evans of Richmond, Virginia, the sleek and efficient Flex-i-File was right at the cutting edge of modern office design, arriving alongside the steel desk and the IBM Electromatic typewriter. The mechanism, which takes its inspiration from the Lazy Tongs corkscrew, stretches and contracts according to how much paper is stored in it. And, as a single slot fits up to 500 sheets of paper, it can hold an awful lot. Today the Flex-i-File is made of recycled aluminum.

WHY IT WORKS: Accommodating and adjustable
WHERE TO GET IT: staples.com, dwr.com

65 Ian Mankin Furnishing Fabrics

Ian Mankin's love of utilitarian fabric may have come from the fabric shop his father owned in London's Soho that sold denim, unbleached calico, and butcher stripes. When visiting John Spencer Textiles' cotton mill in Lancashire, Mankin spotted a cream flannelette with a red stripe running through it that reminded him of a rifle-cleaning cloth he used in his army days. He ordered it and called it Rifle Stripe, and a partnership was born. Incorporating many softer, more colorful interpretations of the traditional mattress ticking stripe, Ian Mankin fabrics continue to be made by John Spencer.

WHY IT WORKS: There's no such thing as too much ticking
WHERE TO GET IT: ianmankin.co.uk

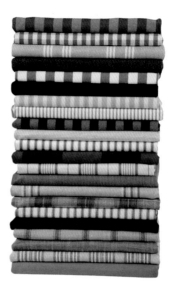

66 Studioilse Bench

Part of the Seating for Eating collection designed in collaboration with the Portuguese furniture company De La Espada, this reinvention of the lowly bench is, in the words of Studioilse, "reassuringly familiar but carefully detailed." Ilse Crawford—style guru, tastemaker, designer, and founder of Studioilse (as well as *Elle Decor*)—finishes the walnut or chestnut design with Danish oil and copper feet. Perfect for the dining room or front hall, it's as versatile as it is beautiful.

WHY IT WORKS: Multipurpose elegance
WHERE TO GET IT: thefutureperfect.com, hivemodern.com

67 Kitchen Serving Set by Jasper Morrison

In his quest to clean up the kitchen, Jasper Morrison has pared down the usual overgrown collection of spoons to three essentials: the multitasking kitchen spoon, the slightly curved risotto serving spoon, and the spatula. Each is 12½ inches in length and made of beech, with holes in the handles for easy hanging.

WHY IT WORKS: Versatile wood spoons
WHERE TO GET IT: allmodern.com

68 Jeeves Coatrack

Sallying forth to put an end to the headache of front hall chaos, the diminutive Jeeves coatrack provides five coat hooks, three key hooks, a mirror, and a shelf for miscellanea. It's designed in the East End of London by design duo Kay + Stemmer, and made of sturdy European oak.

WHY IT WORKS: Space-saving catchall
WHERE TO GET IT: dwr.com

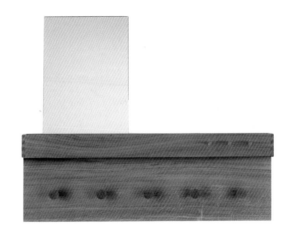

69 Norfolk Willow Log Basket

Intrigued by the wide variety of traditional baskets he saw at a Norfolk, England, market in the 1980s, Adrian Charlton gave up his job on an oil rig to become a basket weaver. His company now cultivates about forty varieties of willow at Burgh-next-Aylsham. No two baskets are alike, and in addition to log baskets, the company makes mushroom foragers, Irish potato skibs, apple cobs, and herring crans. Embraced by Divertimenti and Colefax & Fowler among others, the Norfolk Basket Company is no backwater weaver.

WHY IT WORKS: Deeply stylish tradition
WHERE TO GET IT: norfolkbaskets.co.uk

70 Pia Wallén Cross Blanket

The cross, or crux, is a Swedish folk art symbol for the place where heaven meets earth, and the Pia Wallén cross blanket inspires such passion that it might be the place where heaven and earth actually overlap. The design has until recently been available only to a select group. Sheared, spun, and woven on a small farm in Sweden, the blankets retailed at an extraordinary price, selling out at Skandium before they'd arrived. Now they are made with Swedish flannel and cotton sourced from Peru, making them more affordable for all.

WHY IT WORKS: Positively coveted Scandinavian style
WHERE TO GET IT: store.mjolk.ca

71 Cable Turtle

The Cable Turtle is a modern device created to solve a modern conundrum. Ever since televisions lost their bunny ears, man has been tackling the problem of excess electrical cables lying in wait to trip us up in the office and at home. In 1997 Dutch designer Jan Hoekstra came up with a very simple solution made from that other modern problem, discarded plastic. The donut-like device is basically a spool with a flexible shell that encloses the cable once it's wrapped around the spool. Its brightly colored Dutch minimalist aesthetics have ensured the cable turtle's place in design history, elevating it from humble office device to a spot in the Museum of Modern Art's permanent collection.

WHY IT WORKS: Discreet organization made with recycled materials
WHERE TO GET IT: cableturtle.com

72 Fiskars Scissors

Although these scissors are relatively young, they were created in the oldest steel-forging factory in Finland, founded in 1649. Fiskars' plastic-handled scissors were introduced as a more lightweight and comfortable alternative to the usual forged scissors. The easy-to-find-in-a-messy-drawer color came about when the prototype was made from a leftover resin used for an orange juicer and, by popular demand, was kept.

WHY THEY WORK: Sharp blade and distinctive orange handle
WHERE TO GET THEM: fiskars.com

73 Sawkille Tremper Rabbit Chair

Sawkille Co., a design collective based in New York's Hudson Valley, is committed to reinterpreting farmhouse furniture. Using only the wood of local fallen trees, Sawkille has adopted traditional furniture-building techniques to create what it refers to as rural American design. The Tremper Rabbit chair takes the country kitchen chair to a new level of sophistication, with a dark stain to accentuate its sleek and sculpted silhouette.

WHY IT WORKS: Rural American design in a new package
WHERE TO GET IT: sawkille.com

74 Ørskov Glassware

In 1953 Torben Ørskov, a sort of Danish Terence Conran, opened an eponymous design collective with established industrial designers. Their manifesto was to create affordable, functional, and beautiful household objects: "design classics of the future" that shook the dust off traditional Danish design. Ørskov glasses are made with handblown lab glass, which gives them a deceptively delicate demeanor but a tough resistance to thermal shock. Oven- and microwave-proof, these perfectly perpendicular glasses can be used equally well for wine or hot drinks, like tea and coffee.

WHY IT WORKS: Thin yet surprisingly tough
WHERE TO GET IT: aplusrstore.com

75 Haws Watering Can

Bringing to mind Beatrix Potter's Mr. McGregor, the Haws watering can is proof that the Victorians were capable of designing household objects without flourish. Interested only in functionality, John Haws created a watering can that was all about balance and ease of pouring. In so doing, he also inadvertently created an object of beauty that has not been altered to this day.

WHY IT WORKS: Well-balanced and beautiful
WHERE TO GET IT: bosmereusa.com, kaufmann-mercantile.com

76 Bamboo Ironing Board

An antique wooden ironing board is worth grabbing if ever spotted; its tall, slender shape can do double duty as a dining room sideboard or an extra surface in the kitchen. A metal ironing board just wouldn't do for anything except ironing. West Elm Market's bamboo ironing board with adjustable height is, therefore, a very welcome addition to any room.

WHY IT WORKS: Old-fashioned practicality in a wooden package
WHERE TO GET IT: westelm.com

77 Wüsthof Knife

Before Wüsthof Dreizackwerk decided to rethink the kitchen knife in 1886, cutting into food was a dangerous proposition, as the blade was liable to snap off or detach from the handle. By extending the steel all the way through the handle and sandwiching it between two pieces of wood, Wüsthof Dreizackwerk conceived a new type of knife. Thanks to three distinctive rivets that secured the metal to the wood, there was no longer a need for welding—or fear at the cutting board and table. The riveted design remains unchanged.

WHY IT WORKS: Strong and reliable
WHERE TO GET IT: metrokitchen.com, cutleryandmore.com

78 Ikea Bekväm Stepladder

A new Ikea classic, this beech-wood three-step ladder folds for easy storage, and includes a hook for hanging, Shaker-style.

WHY IT WORKS: A step up from the common step stool
WHERE TO GET IT: ikea.com

79 Hudson's Bay Blanket

In 1780 Cotswold wool blankets were introduced from England as a means to barter with the Native Americans for beaver pelts, buffalo coats, and moccasins. This trading system was facilitated by the Hudson's Bay Company in Canada, a sort of halfway point between the two countries. Fifty years later, John Rich built a mill in Pennsylvania and called it Woolrich, and eight generations later, Woolrich is still the sole purveyor of true Hudson's Bay blankets in America.

WHY IT WORKS: A contemporary-looking classic with ties to America's early history
WHERE TO GET IT: woolrich.com, oldfaithfulshop.com

80 El Casco Stapler

Begun as a gun manufacturer in the Basque region of Spain, El Casco broadened its range to desk accessories in 1934. While the guns have since disappeared, the same care and precision go into its staplers, which are still assembled by hand at a factory run by the founders' grandchildren.

WHY IT WORKS: The Clark Gable of office equipment
WHERE TO GET IT: kaufmann-mercantile.com, wingtip.com, drygoodsny.com

81 Burgon & Ball Gardening Tools

Established several centuries ago in Sheffield and acknowledged as one of the greatest sheep shear companies in the world, Burgon & Ball also makes a range of gardening tools. Using its experience with durable tools and blades, the company produces gardening implements that are sharp, effective, and useful for myriad tasks. Don't just take our word for it: many of Burgon & Ball's tools are endorsed by the Royal Horticultural Society.

WHY THEY WORK: Made to last a lifetime
WHERE TO GET THEM: shovelandhoe.com

82 Mason Cash Mixing Bowls

With an exterior the color and texture of an English custard cream biscuit, the Mason Cash bowl has been a staple of every good British kitchen since Mrs. Beeton wielded a rolling pin. The embossed pattern is not merely decorative: it provides a good grip, and the wide, shallow bowl is ideal for kneading dough. Designed for easy storage, five bowls of varying sizes can be stacked in the space of one.

WHY THEY WORK: Victorian mixing bowls that look at home in the modern kitchen
WHERE TO GET THEM: pacificmerchants.com, cookingandtableware.com

83 Josef Hoffmann Wine Coaster

Standing at the crossroad of Secessionism and the Bauhaus, this nickel-plated coaster is both a useful tabletop accessory and a lesson in design history. Josef Hoffmann created it just after he launched the Wiener Werkstätte with artist Koloman Moser in 1903. The workshops represented a shared vision between craftsmen and designers, and produced furniture, textiles, glass, and ceramics, as well as metalwork. The stacked rows of square windows in the coaster can be seen in Hoffmann's furniture and in the architecture of the period, and reflect the influence of Charles Rennie Mackintosh.

WHY IT WORKS: A drip catcher that's dripping in history
WHERE TO GET IT: neuegalerie.org

84 Another Country Three-Legged Stool

Taking its inspiration from the Shakers as well as from Japanese and Scandinavian woodwork, London-based design firm Another Country has focused its attention on furniture archetypes. It has reassessed the humble three-legged stool with a cool eye, granting its FSC oak design clean lines and a contemporary finish that allow it to double as a bedside or side table, as well as provide a welcome seat.

WHY IT WORKS: A modern take on a once overlooked piece of furniture
WHERE TO GET IT: anothercountry.com

85 Coir and Wire Doormat

Coir, a fiber made from the outer husk of a coconut and used for making ropes as well as matting, is combined with wire to effectively scrape off mud while resisting moisture. This doormat is handmade in India with an underside of recycled rubber.

WHY IT WORKS: Natural and long-lasting
WHERE TO GET IT: wayfair.com

86 Puukko Knife Rack by Uusi

Although the magnetized Puukko knife rack is sleek and modern in appearance, its wood is rather ancient. Reclaimed from early-twentieth-century Chicago water towers, the cypress and redwood were already about three hundred years old when they were milled. That means Galileo was looking up at the stars when these trees began their lives. The knife rack was created by the Chicago-based design duo Linnea Gits and Peter Dunham of Uusi.

WHY IT WORKS: A magnetic knife rack with a hidden history
WHERE TO GET IT: uusi.us

87 Best Made Cloth-Covered Extension Cord

Until now, the extension cord has followed the Henry Ford ethic: any color as long as it's black (or brown). It took a graphic designer to turn this lowly household object into a cause for celebration. Why shouldn't an extension cord be covered in red or yellow or candy-striped cloth? And for that matter, why shouldn't it be made in the USA? With the same design principles he used to transform the axe into an object of beauty, Peter Buchanan Smith of Best Made Company has pulled this necessary but ugly object out of the dark corner and into the spotlight.

WHY IT WORKS: An extension cord that need not be hidden
WHERE TO GET IT: bestmadeco.com

88 Libeco Linen

Based in the Flanders region of Belgium, which has been producing fabric since the thirteenth century, Libeco is all about linen. Its industrial process involves its own vocabulary of retting, scotching, and hackling. The resulting fabric is hypoallergenic, thermo-regulating, and long-lasting. It is also very attractive, especially in Libeco's collection of linen tea towels and cooking aprons.

WHY IT WORKS: A natural fabric that improves with age
WHERE TO GET IT: libecohomestores.com

89 Pawleys Island Hammock

A consolation prize for Christopher Columbus's not finding Japan in 1492 was his discovery of the rope hammock, which he brought back from the Bahamas. Thought up by islanders as a way to get a good night's sleep while suspended above the peril of snakes and insects, the hammock was later adopted by the British navy for use on the high seas. At the end of the eighteenth century, a Southern riverboat captain known as Cap'n Josh decided to add a slat from an oak barrel to each end of the hammock to create a flat bed of woven rope. He preferred this method of sleeping—and so did his neighbors. The hammocks are still woven in Cap'n Josh's hometown of Pawleys Island, South Carolina.

WHY IT WORKS: Structured for extended loafing
WHERE TO GET IT: pawleysislandhammocks.com

90 Slack Dry Mop

Assembled by hand in Vermont using wool carpet remnants from the South and recycled poplar wood from the North, this wool dry mop is a uniquely American invention, patented by Alexander P. Slack in 1909 and originally sold door-to-door by his seven sons (the company is still family-run). The secret to its enduring success is that the lanolin in the wool "draws dust like a magnet," according to Tom Slack III, and holds it until the mop is shaken out.

WHY IT WORKS: Century-old design that combats dust, lint, and dirt
WHERE TO GET IT: kaufmann-mercantile.com, westelm.com

91 Bayco Clip Lamp

Harking back to the days when the hardware store was a treasure trove of tin lunch boxes, wooden clothespins, and rubber galoshes, the aluminum light continues to bring instant illumination. With its 150-watt bulb capacity, adjustable ball joint for positioning, and steel clamp, the unassuming clip lamp is equally at home at a building site, in a painter's studio, or in a loft.

WHY IT WORKS: Versatile movable light
WHERE TO GET IT: homedepot.com and hardware stores nationwide

92 Old English Sheffield Silver Cutlery

The William Turner workroom has been making cutlery in Sheffield, England, since 1887. This style, known as Old English, dates back to about 1750, when the Georgians were producing their own form of minimalist design in architecture, landscaping, and furniture. There has never been any reason to update or change these shapes, and so they have been left alone and confidently take their place in any traditional or contemporary table setting.

WHY IT WORKS: Georgian timeless minimalism
WHERE TO GET IT: williamturnersheffield.com

93 Jacob Bromwell Colander

Jacob Bromwell began his housewares business in the frontier town of Cincinnati, Ohio, in 1819. The Bromwell Brush & Wire Goods Company catered to homesteaders by selling tin cups, corn poppers, flour sifters, rat traps, and other necessities. About a century later, the company introduced its iconic star-patterned aluminum colander, a lightweight drainer footed for placement on a countertop. Used for rinsing produce and for draining pasta, the colanders are still made in the United States in small batches, and Bromwell's descendants still run the company.

WHY IT WORKS: Ageless star-spangled kitchen utensil
WHERE TO GET IT: jacobbromwell.com

94 Burnside Light

Although deceptively simple and understated in form, the Burnside light is a collaborative project between manufacturer and customer, assembled at Rejuvenation in Portland, Oregon. The customer selects from a range of socket finishes, cloth-cord colors, and lengths, as well as canopy colors. And if a shade is required, there is a variety of colors and materials to choose from. The process is a delicious dilemma of choices and provides an unexpected but welcome lesson in interior design.

WHY IT WORKS: Design-it-yourself illumination
WHERE TO GET IT: rejuvenation.com

95 Thomas Hoof Toilet Roll Holder

German designer Thomas Hoof, founder of European household mecca Manufactum.com and creator of Thomas Hoof Produkt, is a hardware visionary. Taking classic lighting fixtures, switches, doorknobs, and faucets, he reinterprets them for the twenty-first century using trim silhouettes and well-crafted materials. Though we're hard-pressed to pick a favorite from the lineup, the toilet roll holder gets our vote. Made of porcelain, it's a laughably simple design: a slim toilet roll is placed in the cavity and the paper is pulled down through a slot. No wood or plastic necessary.

WHY IT WORKS: Satisfying simplicity
WHERE TO GET IT: produktgesellschaft.de, manufactum.com

96 Sheepskin Rug

The sheepskin rug, so often seen in the nursery in its shorn, cream-colored state, takes on a new attitude when the wool is left long or the hides are taken from mottled heritage breeds. The latter is difficult to find in America, but Toast in the U.K. provides a good variety of sheepskins that can be draped over the back of a chair or used as a rug.

WHY IT WORKS: A familiar hide with a rustic twist
WHERE TO GET IT: toast.co.uk

97 Danforth Pewter Oil Lamp

Before the Civil War, American households relied on pewter for all their tabletop needs, and Thomas Danforth II was the pioneering spearhead of the pewter age. Today, his descendants continue this tradition with a pewter workshop in Middlebury, Vermont. Assembled by hand with lead-free pewter, the Mariner model oil lamp is inspired by a ship's decanter, slender at the top and wide at the base to prevent tipping.

WHY IT WORKS: Hurricane-proof elegance
WHERE TO GET IT: canoeonline.net

98 Wire Flyswatter

As effective as the unsightly bright blue or green plastic flyswatter, but altogether more attractive and tidy. When this German-made swatter constructed with wire and beech wood makes contact with the fly, it gives a little, so the fly kindly removes itself from the wall after impact.

WHY IT WORKS: The nonsquash swat
WHERE TO GET IT: manufactum.com

99 Enamel Soap Dish

Nothing suggests utility chic quite like enamelware, once ubiquitous in every household. Porcelain enamel, a form of ground glass and pigment, was applied to iron or steel to protect it from rust while providing an affordable alternative to porcelain. Enamel was used to coat all manner of objects, from buckets to roasting tins. Its popularity declined steeply after the advent of plastic, but a few companies still make it today and have been prudent in not altering the original designs. This pleasingly old-world soap dish hails from Germany; it has a removable base that drains into the bowl, preventing the soap from getting soggy.

WHY IT WORKS: Self-draining and elegant
WHERE TO GET IT: kioskkiosk.com

100 Weck Mold Jar

Before J. Weck was established, fruit preservation depended largely on the use of alcohol, a problem for teetotaler Johann Carl Weck. He lived in Baden, Germany, an area abundant with orchards, and so the question of fruit preservation was frequently on his mind. Then he came upon a patent from a local chemist who discovered that by boiling a jar and sealing it with rubber and a weighted-down lid, one could avoid the use of booze altogether. Weck bought the patent and joined up with a talented salesman, who added the strawberry logo, one of the earliest trademarks in Germany and still in use today, along with Weck's signature metal clips.

WHY IT WORKS: A preserves jar that doubles as a storage container
WHERE TO GET IT: weckjars.com, kaufmann-mercantile.com

Remodeling Reality

*You've heard the horror stories: projects that
drag on for months, even years, past the projected
finish dates. Budget overruns that drain bank
accounts. Couples that split up the minute they cross
the threshold of their newly remodeled abodes.
Trust us, it doesn't have to be this way.*

*Among us we've been through more than a dozen
remodels. Miraculously, we've survived the
financial strain, we're friends with our architects,
and we sing the praises of our contractors. If that
sounds smug, we'll admit that luck had a lot to do
with it. But the results have been so life-changing
that we're inspired to share our strategies
with you in hopes of making your own experience
less daunting. Remodeling is messy and arduous.
But it can also be transformative, an aesthetic
journey you'll never regret.*

By Meredith Swinehart

01

Before You Begin

Size up your project by asking yourself these crucial questions. The more informed you are about what you're getting into, the smoother and speedier the process will be.

IS IT WORTH IT?

Most successful remodeling stories begin with a house or an apartment that shows underlying promise: what decorators like to call "good bones." Look beyond misguided paint choices and ugly carpeting for well-proportioned rooms that flow well from one to the next—or, at least, present signs of possibility, such as an open-plan living/dining space in an otherwise forgettable ranch house. If you are considering buying a place with the intent to remodel, do not pass go without getting the advice of an architect and a contractor. Many offer this service gratis, hoping that a job will follow. They will provide insights into what's possible, how much it will cost, and whether the project is worthwhile. If your goal is a complete overhaul, keep in mind that it's cheaper and easier in the long run to shoulder one big remodel than to break the work into stages. And before you make any moves, consider leaving things "as is" for a few months. It's enormously helpful to test-drive a house before you fix it.

WHERE WILL YOU LIVE DURING THE PROJECT?

Remodeling is noisy, chaotic, and, above all, dusty. If you're doing a minor update (a small bathroom, for instance), it's fine to stay put. But if you're doing a major overhaul, consider renting a place nearby or offering your services as a house sitter.

HOW DO YOU WANT TO LIVE?

Think of remodeling as an opportunity to define your aesthetic. Whether or not you enlist the help of an interior designer, take time to size up your likes and dislikes and establish priorities. Most important, trust your instincts. As designer Ellen Hamilton says, "It's a pitfall to think that the design professional knows better than the homeowner in matters of taste. To get the best results, it's important for the person who's going to be living in the space to know his or her own mind."

HOW TO BEGIN?

Gather images of rooms that speak to you. Remodelista is an ideal resource; so are other websites (see our site's Design Newsstand), books, magazines, and the world at large. Build your design files online with sites like Pinterest, Tumblr, or Evernote, which make it easy to add targeted captions, or with hard copies pinned to a mood board or stashed in a folder. Look for themes in your selections, and winnow out anything that on a second or third glance doesn't hold up.

Steep yourself in your stuff. What is and isn't working for you now? What would you hate to see go? Pay attention to your patterns and habits. You might dislike the way your current kitchen cabinets look but love the ease with which they open.

Make a list of your priorities and goals, and refer to it often. Where is it important to spend a little extra to get what you're after? And where can you save? Aim to consolidate the former and expand the latter. For example, splurge on customized built-in storage and save by buying furniture on sale and at Ikea. Or use marble in the master bath but subway tile in all the others.

Think long-term. Consider how your needs will change over time, and keep your options open. Today's playroom could become tomorrow's home office. The nursery will one day morph into a teenager's room. And the extra bathroom just may be the laundry room of your dreams.

PRO TIP

Dream Big

Begin by coming up with a plan that gives you everything you want. True, you may have to scale back on scope and first-choice materials, but the exercise allows you to establish the look and feel that you're after. And it gives you a good sense of what things cost.

TODD NICKEY, designer, Nickey Kehoe, Los Angeles

02

A Realistic Budget

Controlling expenses is the most daunting part of any remodel; when you're in the thick of it, it can feel as though you're shoveling money into your house. Here's how to spare yourself and your bank account.

WHAT WILL IT COST?

Gathering information up front, before a Dumpster is on the horizon, is your best route forward and can help keep plans in perspective.

Talk to an architect or a contractor. Get an idea early on of what your project may cost. (Unless you intend to hire that architect or contractor, pay for the consultation.)

Consider how long you plan to stay in your house. Will your improvements pay for themselves over the long run? (A contractor can help you answer this.)

Get some friendly advice. If a friend has tackled a similar project, ask her about her total expenditure—and then add 50 percent (as a form of self-preservation, people always forget at least half the costs).

Start researching improvements. Spend time looking at the many levels of available finishes, cabinets, plumbing fixtures, lighting, and appliances, so you'll be better informed about quality versus cost.

Set aside a slush fund. There are almost always going to be unpleasant surprises when remodeling, and the bigger the project, the more expensive the surprises will be. We suggest banking at least 10 percent of your budget as a contingency in case things go wrong. This fund should not be used to indulge your sudden requirement for a built-in dressing room; it's there to cover design and technical overruns.

Beware Cost-Per-Square-Foot Calculations

These calculations are almost worthless, because there is no standard for what's included in that number. Is architecture? How about building permits? Landscaping? Contractors' fees? The other pitfall is that you have no idea if you're comparing apples with apples. If someone builds a house on a hillside, it will cost more than a house on a flat lot. A kitchen might cost $1,000 per square foot and a kid's bedroom $100 per square foot. Consequently, using a cost-per-square-foot number to determine your budget is only valid in a very broad sense.

RICH TINCHER, contractor,
Tincher Construction, Redwood City, California

03

Where to Spend, Where to Save

All of us at Remodelista subscribe to a high/low approach to design: We mix favorite pricey things with accessible, affordable ones. And we see beauty in any well-designed object, whether it's from a rarefied boutique or the corner hardware store.

15 THINGS WORTH SPENDING ON

❶ Architecture.
Spend on achieving timeless designs built to last. Plenty of natural light and outdoor views are nice, too. It's no coincidence that your biggest expenses offer the biggest payback.

❷ Craftsmanship.
If you value high-quality work and have an eye for details, there is no way to cut corners here.

❸ Structural integrity and energy efficiency.
Spend to ensure that your foundation, roof, windows, heating systems, and insulation are sound and working properly. Adding extra insulation in walls and ceilings will reduce energy consumption.

❹ A well-designed landscape.
The benefits of living amid well-tended plants include the aesthetic (flowers and shrubs make everything look better), the environmental (think of every sprout as an air filter), and the therapeutic (if you're a gardener, you know what we're talking about). And it needn't be demanding; a low-maintenance landscape can do the trick.

❺ Exterior materials.
Houses have to be able to stand up to the elements. Water damage is especially unforgiving, so get to know your gutters and keep up with paint and roofing maintenance.

❻ The kitchen.
If you love to cook or are feeding a family, a great kitchen is not only life-enhancing but life-changing. Conversely, if you eat out for every meal, no need to splurge on a fancy range.

❼ Good lighting.
A combination of ambient and directed lighting is far preferable to ceiling blasters. Multiple light sources improve a room. Fixtures don't have to be expensive, but they should be well made (hardware-store porcelain sockets fit the bill). When walls are being opened up, seize the opportunity to add built-in fixtures, and don't hold back—it's much more expensive to make these additions later.

❽ Custom millwork and cabinetry.
If you intend to stay put for a long time, it's worth spending to get exactly what you want. Built-ins enable you to live clutter-free and make the most of your space.

❾ Door and cabinet hardware.
Think about the number of times a day you will touch these pieces. They should look and feel good and function well.

❿ Plumbing.
Faucets and other plumbing fixtures need not be expensive, but they should perform well—steer clear of cheaply made options.

⓫ Solid wood doors.
Consider their acoustic properties—both the sound they make when they close and the sounds they block from room to room.

⓬ Your sofa.
Of all your furnishings, the couch gets used, and abused, the most. Pay for one that's well-made and comfortable and looks great in your space (and if it's floating in the room, make sure the back is as presentable as the front).

⓭ The best painter you can afford.
A masterful paint job makes everyone's work look great. But feel free to scrimp if you have young kids—your impeccable walls won't last long anyway.

⓮ A great front door and well-detailed arrival space.
First impressions have a big impact. And it's very nice to come home after a long day to a place that feels right.

⓯ Things that make life easier.
Assess your day-to-day needs and take action. If you find yourself doing laundry all the time, treat yourself to an accessible, high-functioning setup (for a good idea, see page 203). And if you wish your family would hang up their coats, bags, and keys, adding wall hooks could be a game changer.

15 WAYS TO SAVE

❶ Minimize square footage.
Double up on utility and avoid having seldom-used spaces, like formal dining and living rooms.

❷ Embrace mundane materials.
The most expensive finishes often require the most maintenance. Save money by avoiding both and embracing honest, hardworking basics like concrete floors, subway tiles, and butcher-block counters.

❸ Repeat yourself.
Ordering small quantities of a variety of things adds up (think freight and service charges for each). You can negotiate a better price by buying in quantity—and your rooms will look more unified if you carry over the same materials, such as moldings and hardware, throughout.

❹ Don't overspend on static items.
There is a huge variety of options when it comes to tile, moldings, and wall finishes. You don't have to succumb to the high end: subway tile is less than $2 per square foot and can be used in countless ways.

❺ Use luxurious accents.
Think marble tile backsplash instead of sheet marble countertops. You'll get the desired effect while keeping costs down.

❻ Avoid luxury woods.
Instead use affordable, sustainable varieties, like white pine, and stain them.

❼ Reassess your need for fancy technology.
It will go the way of last year's laptop.

❽ Swap out pricey peripherals.
When functionality won't be affected, opt for practicality. If you long for a zinc roof, consider an aluminum one painted in a zinc tone.

❾ Acquire furnishings as you can afford them.
Buy fewer things and keep them for the long haul. Instead of filling your house up all at once, gather as you go—especially if you see the right piece at the right price.

❿ Scrimp on secondary areas.
Utility rooms, pantries, and extra bathrooms can be well designed inexpensively (see "The Under $500 Powder Room," page 121). Spend on what you'll see and use the most.

⓫ Preserve old details.
Rather than replacing the original, the worn, and the interesting, live with it. Case in point: and Robert Highsmith and Stefanie Brechbuehler's newfangled old kitchen (pages 54–55) and Justine Hand's spatter-painted floors (page 273).

⓬ Scavenge for salvaged materials.
We're all for shopping the sidewalks on garbage days (but beware of bedbugs). When using found materials, such as old cabinets, keep in mind that while they may add to your labor costs, you'll reduce your environmental footprint.

⓭ Shop locally.
European manufacturers may have just the lights and doorknobs you're after. But they're likely to cost extra, take forever to arrive, and require parts that aren't available here.

⓮ Don't keep up with the Joneses.
Review potential appliances and materials with fresh eyes. Is a brand name really needed? How about a Jenn-Air fridge instead of a Sub-Zero, or Andersen windows instead of Marvin? Go with whatever meets your needs for the best price.

⓯ Consider the life cycle of objects.
It's worth paying more for quality. Things made to last cost you less in the long run.

Where to Spend, Where to Save

Remodeling Reality

04

The Details

The design world and the magazines that cover it tend to be tight-lipped about resources and trade secrets. We're out to break down the walls of exclusivity. Everything that goes into your house deserves your careful consideration, and at Remodelista we're all about sharing sources and demystifying design. Before you finalize your plans, consider these options.

FRILLS WORTH CONSIDERING

If your remodel budget can support it, here are some extras you won't regret adding:

A fireplace or wood stove. Not only for heat, but as a focal point.

Pull-out shelving in kitchen cabinets. An efficient way to make the most of your storage space.

Two dishwashers. If you entertain all the time or have a big family, it makes sense to double your cleaning power.

Antifog bathroom mirrors. You'll be able to see yourself, of course, and even shave while you shower.

Acoustic insulation for bathrooms. Particularly advisable if your dining table is next to the powder room.

Dimmers on the light switches. Combat harsh lighting and save energy.

Self-closing cabinet drawers. Built-in tidiness is hugely satisfying.

An electronics charging station. You'll never have to search for an outlet again.

Interior shutters. Shutters are an architectural alternative to curtains and shades.

Designated area for your pets' things. Factor your pets' needs into the design plan, so you don't have to go looking for a spot to hide the kitty litter box and the dog crate.

A waist-high dog-washing tub. This is a true luxury for long-legged owners.

DESIGN TRICKS THAT WORK

As you plan your remodel, consider trying these approaches to transforming a space:

Raise window and door heights to make rooms feel taller and views more expansive.

Use one floor finish throughout the home to blur boundaries between rooms and visually enlarge the space.

Choose natural materials and finishes; they wear better over time.

Swap ugly plastic light switch plates with metal or ceramic ones for an instant room upgrade.

Introduce odd couples, such as a humble tin container on a marble counter, to create visual tension and interest.

Be mindful of the tiniest of details—choices like copper nails and slotted screws telegraph a finished look.

BUDGET-SAVING STORES

As a rule, we prefer to support small workshops and the stores that stock their wares. We're against sweatshop goods and throwaway consumerism. That said, on occasion even the most discerning among us turn to the big chains like Ikea and Home Depot for affordable, well-made basics. But we avoid items that require high-grade materials or a lot of moving parts (they fall apart), and instead zero in on serviceable staples.

What to buy at Ikea	What to avoid at Ikea	What to buy at a home improvement chain	What to avoid at a home improvement chain
Partyware (such as bulk wineglasses)	Plumbing fixtures	Basic building materials (lumber, fasteners, adhesives, etc.)	Wood, other than basic construction lumber
Children's furniture	Flooring	All but the cheapest lines of plumbing fixtures and fittings	Anything that would be hard to remove from your home down the line, such as built-in lighting
Butcher block	Mattresses, pillows, and sheets	Prefinished flooring	Refined materials like bathroom vanities, designer hardware, and kitchen systems
Rugs	Lighting with fine parts	Basic ceramic tile	Cabinetry
Accessories in stainless steel, glass, and ceramic	Furniture for high-use areas	Plants and planting materials	Lighting fixtures
Some curtain fabrics (first make sure they're opaque enough for your needs)	Items with moving parts		
Metal hardware (avoid plastic)			
Cabinets, especially the Abstrakt line			
LED lighting			

Imported Fixtures Aren't Worth It (Usually)

Be especially wary of expensive products from companies based outside of your home country. The only exceptions I would make to this rule are some top brands that really work well. Vola and Dornbracht faucets are expensive but do what they say they will. Dinesen floors likewise. Such is the value of working with a designer or architect who knows their brands and can ensure that you outfit your home with trusted, long-lasting products.

MIKE RUNDELL, architect,
MRJ Rundell + Associates, London

05

Environmentally Friendly Options

The greenest choice you can make when remodeling is to think small. Assess how much space you really need and stop there. Beyond that, it is almost always more sustainable to repair and reuse materials than it is to replace them (even if it's not always the most affordable approach).

If you do decide to swap out materials and appliances, consider the long and growing list of eco-friendly models and choose new materials that (where possible) are locally sourced, recycled (and recyclable), and enduring. Some purchases to consider:

Radiant-heat flooring.
An effective, efficient, and affordable alternative to radiators and forced air.

Instantaneous hot-water heaters.
These tankless setups are energy savers (no hot water sitting in a tank waiting to be used); they have a longer life span than their giant counterparts, but also less capacity.

Ample window shades.
Like hats, they hold in the heat.

Solar hot water and photovoltaic panels.
Energy, free for the taking.

Wood certified to be sustainably harvested.
See the Forest Stewardship Council site, usfsc.org, for information and a list of retailers.

Easy-to-use trash areas.
To encourage your household to recycle and compost.

Carpet with natural fibers.
Hard-wearing with no off-gassing.

Formaldehyde-free cabinets and furniture.
A known carcinogen, formaldehyde is used as an adhesive in composite woods; instead, opt for designs made from solid wood or formaldehyde-free plywood.

Cellulose or cotton blown-in insulation made from recycled paper.
The green alternative to fiberglass batting. It can save you up to 30 percent on fuel costs.

Stone exterior materials.
They'll last an eternity.

A light-colored roof.
Your house will be cooler than with a dark roof.

Natural ventilation through high clerestory windows.
A fresh cross breeze is the ideal substitute for air-conditioning.

Metal siding.
It's weatherproof and, unlike vinyl siding, looks good, too.

Low-flow toilets and fixtures.
Prevent water waste.

Energy-miser light fixtures and LED bulbs.
Prevent energy waste.

Lighting controls and occupant sensors.
Ensure that when rooms are empty, the lights are out.

06

The Team

It can be hard to know whether you need to hire an architect or a designer for your remodel or whether your contractor or carpenter can manage it solo. You may be tempted to try a project yourself but wonder if you have the time and the ability—or whether a handy friend might do a better job. At Remodelista, we're fans of all approaches. Design professionals are invaluable assets in a remodel, but we understand the appeal of going it alone. Here, some insight into choosing your crew.

THE ARCHITECT

Architects are highly trained professionals adept at design work, structural solutions, and construction management; it's their job to help you articulate a holistic vision for the project. Opt for full service, and your architect will not only devise an overall scheme, allowing you to be as involved in the process as you want, but will also:

Provide all the necessary construction drawings.

Source key materials to be purchased by the contractor, including stone and tile, plumbing, and lighting.

Secure all necessary permits.

Ensure the project's structural soundness.

Oversee the building process from start to finish, working with the general contractor to manage all the problems, delays, and choices that arise along the way.

In other words, you get a lot for your money. But as a way to trim costs, you can also hire an architect on a more limited basis (see "What It Costs," opposite).

DO YOU REALLY NEED AN ARCHITECT?

As a general rule of thumb, you should consider hiring an architect if any of these conditions apply:

The projected cost of the remodel is over $25,000.

Drawings are needed to obtain building permits and/or to show your contractor exactly how to construct something.

You are reorganizing spaces and moving walls, or doing any other task that requires an overall design concept as well as attention to structural integrity.

Your local authorities require projects of a particular size and scope to be handled by a registered architect. Check with your building department.

Still in doubt? Interview a few architects, being clear that you are in the preliminary stages of a project and deciding if you need professional help. Most will candidly assess the scope of work and let you know whether their involvement is required.

WHAT IT COSTS

Architectural fees vary but average about 15 percent of the cost of construction. That can be more than worthwhile, particularly when you consider the money you'll be saving in potential errors of judgment from inexperience. An architect's management can also speed construction, saving you money if you're paying double rent or mortgage while construction is under way. Most important, a design pro will come up with spatial solutions and materials you would otherwise not have found. If your budget is tight, many architects will work with you on a limited basis—to generate design and construction drawings, for instance, or to create a set of drawings solely for the purpose of getting a building permit. If you take one of these approaches, however, you and your general contractor will be on your own as questions crop up—and they always do—during the construction phase. And the demanding role of project administrator will be yours.

FINDING THE PERFECT MATCH

Leave yourself plenty of time to hire an architect. Most have work scheduled months into the future, and the interviewing process may take you a couple of months. Some basic rules to consider for the search:

Seek out someone whose work you love—and who has designed the kind of living space you're after. If you want a design that's extremely personal to you, look for an architect whose work shows a range of voices. The Remodelista Architect/Designer Directory on our site is a great resource—it offers portfolios of recommended professionals from coast to coast.

Make sure you are in sync. Think about the scope of the project: Does it seem to be right up the architect's alley, a stretch, or not big enough? You want someone to feel fully invested in the job. If you opt to go with a large firm, you risk having your work done by a junior designer rather than the big guns. Also, make sure your communication styles mesh. You'll be in touch with your architect many times a week—sometimes many times a day. If you prefer e-mail or require weekend updates, your architect must be willing to meet those needs.

Get references. Ask former clients: How was the architect to work with? Did the job finish on time and come in within budget? You want to find a professional who gets great word of mouth and has ongoing relationships with clients.

Conduct an interview. The architect-client relationship is like a short-term marriage, so choose someone you genuinely like and feel compatible with. Does she understand your priorities? An architect who is not listening to you in the interview will not listen to you later on. And make sure she communicates well. Is she able to explain design solutions with clarity, avoiding industry jargon, or does she ramble on about her philosophy? The bottom line: you want a collaborator.

Sign a contract. To make sure all expectations are fully spelled out, it behooves you to have a formal agreement. The American Institute of Architects website, AIA.org, offers a range of architect-owner contracts that cover almost every situation that may arise. Be clear about what is covered in the architect's fees and what are considered additional costs, such as creating drawings of the existing conditions as a reference. Also establish who from the firm you'll be dealing with—and make sure that person is the one responsible for your design.

THE INTERIOR DESIGNER

If you want help recasting a room or a whole house, and you don't plan to make major structural changes, hiring a designer is a great option. It often costs less than going with an architect, and it allows you to make over a space—focusing on proportion, color, light, and texture—without bringing in the wrecking ball. Traditionally, architects attend to the bones of a space, while designers flesh it out. These days there's often crossover between their roles. As with architects, designers come up with an overall plan and present it in the form of drawings for the contractor if construction is involved. Designers oversee installation of their work but don't manage construction. (Note that the terms *interior designer* and *decorator* are simply a matter of preference; most of the professionals we work with call themselves designers.)

FINDING THE PERFECT MATCH

There are all manner of designers out there, some with rigorous schooling and credentials (architects who aren't licensed—a complicated process; every state sets its own requirements—call themselves designers), others largely self-taught; some with very particular styles, others more eclectic. Their fees run the gamut from hourly rates to a percentage of the cost of construction. To hire a designer, follow the same guidelines as you would for an architect (see preceding page) and consult the Remodelista Architect/Designer Directory for vetted options from coast to coast. Then meet with more than one professional and ask them to explain their process. Aligning expectations from the start is critical, and will determine whether or not you end up with what you envisioned.

THE CONTRACTOR

So named because they're contracted to get specialized jobs done, contractors are the highly skilled managers on construction sites. There are general contractors, or GCs (also sometimes known as builders or foremen), who oversee the construction process. And then there are subcontractors—plumbers, cabinetmakers, electricians, painters, etc.—who are typically hired and managed by the GC.

FINDING THE PERFECT MATCH

A general contractor should have excellent organizational and time-management abilities, people skills, and experience managing a team. Whether or not you're working with an architect, you will ultimately be responsible for choosing the contractor for your job. Some tips to guide you through the process:

Get recommendations. Referrals can come from your architect or designer, friends, local lumber company, or building department. Finding a great contractor is all about reputation. Make sure that he has experience in the type of project you're doing, and always check to make sure he is licensed and insured.

Do your homework. Any potential GC should be glad to hand over a list of past clients. Call your way through these referrals and read reviews online. Always ask if the project came in on time and within budget.

Assess the GC's work. When possible, check out finished work in person; assess it for both aesthetic quality and craftsmanship.

Conduct an interview. You'll want to find someone who listens to you, communicates well, and—if you are unfamiliar with construction—is able to explain technical concepts and terminology. Also ask about how the GC manages his workload. Will your project have a dedicated team, or will it be rotated in with other jobs? Make sure your expectations in this area are understood.

THE HIRING PROCESS

Before you decide which contractor to go with, you'll need to understand how GCs are hired, because how they quote their work may influence your hiring decision. Contractors can be brought on in two ways: by negotiated contract or competitive bid. A bit of background on both will help you decide which way to go:

Negotiated contract. In this method you invite a general contractor to join your team, and he signs on early in the process, during the design phase. He is paid a percentage of construction costs, usually 15 to 25 percent. With this setup your architect and contractor work in tandem, discussing materials options and weighing the cost of construction for one approach versus another. A merging of the creative and practical sides of the project, the negotiated contract ideally produces the best design outcome at the best price. The downside: there's a lot of planning as you go, which can make it hard to rein in costs.

Competitive bid. You (or your architect) ask two or more contractors to compete for your project, which is meant to secure you the best deal. Each will submit a scope of work and a price for which he'll complete it. The fee is contained in the price. In order to be effective, the competitive bidding process requires a lot of advance work on your end, because you have to outline the project in complete detail to each bidder. Leave something out, and it will cost you later: the dreaded "change order." The downside: competitive bidders have an incentive to overlook or hide costs that aren't explicitly requested. But the most experienced and reputable know that it behooves everyone to be realistic and aboveboard from the get-go. Do not hire the cheapest, fastest contractor, especially if he stands out in a field of higher bids. When it comes to construction, you get what you pay for.

SIGNING A CONTRACT

Once you've agreed to the payment method, put your terms into a legal agreement; we recommend those on the American Institute of Architects website, AIA.org. Make sure it stipulates that the work is to be performed per your specifications (you will likely have to hire an architect or a draftsman to create working drawings) and per the bid provided. It is important that the contract be explicit about details. If paint costs are being covered, for instance, what brand is specified? (Leave it vague, and you'll be stuck with the cheapest brand the contractor can get or have to pay extra for Farrow & Ball.) You can't be too meticulous when it comes to spelling out the scope of work to be done. Include a clause for keeping the site clean and performing work in a timely manner, with some sort of action you may take (such as withholding payment) if this does not occur. Similarly, you will want to include a clause for inadequate work, either requiring that it be repaired to meet the agreed-upon specifications or allowing you to make the repairs and deduct the cost from what the contractor is owed.

07

Team-work

Now that you have assembled your talent, here's how to help it perform like a well-oiled machine. The process actually begins with you: appoint one owner to be the communicator and person who fields daily questions from the site. Which of you is the most decisive, detail-oriented, and available? The job is yours.

HOW TO MAKE TEAMWORK WORK

The architect and/or designer, contractor, and all other crew should have clearly defined roles and be working toward the same goal. What you can do to help:

Know who hires whom. The owner hires the architect, who usually recommends general contractors and specialists, such as interior designers, landscape architects, and structural engineers. The client interviews each of these team members for compatibility and hires them directly. The general contractor recommends, hires, manages, and pays all subcontractors. This hierarchy is critical for both efficiency and quality of work.

Hire people who've worked together before. They will understand one another's styles of communication and working habits and be more likely to successfully collaborate, helping to save time and avoid misunderstandings.

Think twice before bringing in your own subcontractors. As strange as it may sound, adding outsiders to the mix can cause awkwardness and tension. If you want to compile the subs yourself, be prepared for potential compromises in design and/or costs associated with a new team's learning curve.

Building a Successful Team

You will be spending a lot of time with your architect, contractor, plumber, and electrician. You will speak to them more than you do your own family.
I assembled my dream design team the way I hired my team at work— I wanted to be surrounded by the best and brightest in the field.
Above and beyond finding people who came highly qualified and well-recommended, it was key to me to find people who possessed communication skills and the right attitude.

JENNIFER CATTO, owner of a recently
remodeled town house

08

A Few Notes on Doing It Yourself

The rewards of taking on your own remodel are obvious; you will theoretically minimize costs and earn yourself a huge sense of accomplishment. But there are barriers.

Be realistic about how much time you have, and be prepared to spend if things go awry. That old adage "If you want something done right, you have to do it yourself" does not apply when you don't know what you're doing.

If you decide to tackle a big project on your own, first take the time to create an accurate survey of your space. This will save you many headaches down the road. Do you really understand waterproofing, structural loads, live electricity? These things operate by their own rules and are unforgiving—consult an expert.

Remodelista loves DIY, but we suggest you save yourself the frustration and risks by outsourcing all but the smallest projects. Here's a quick guide to help you decide if you want to venture into contractor territory:

Do it yourself	**Consider doing it yourself (if you're really handy)**	**Don't do it yourself**
Painting	Removing and replacing old tile and bathroom fixtures	Electrical work
Installing simple flooring systems	Replacing doors and windows	Plumbing
Installing basic tile	Replacing appliances	Concrete work
Refinishing wood surfaces	Installing prefabricated cabinets	Metalwork
Swapping out hardware	Constructing a simple wooden deck	Installing drywall
Replacing light covers	Small, nonstructural demolition	Structural framing or changing the dimensions of a room
Changing out trim and moldings	Applying plaster finishes	Sanding wood floors or stairs with a lot of corners
Installing off-the-shelf shelving units		
Building basic shelving or utility furniture		

09

The Process

Construction can be a daunting experience, especially if you're going through it for the first time. The best place to start is to ask others (your contractor, architect, fellow remodelers) what to expect, but here are the basic guidelines—and some advice to keep you sane along the way.

STICKING TO YOUR BUDGET

Every remodel has some surprises, but you can minimize them by combating the two biggest threats to a balanced budget—scope creep and change orders.

Scope creep. There is a saying that the four most expensive words in a remodel are "While we're at it." The scope of every project has a tendency to expand. It is deceptively easy for seemingly small improvements to be made one after another, thereby ruining your budget. Be sure that you and your construction team are speaking the same language, and adding things up as you go, in order to avoid a shock when items are tallied.

Change orders. A change order is a written request from the owner or architect to depart from previously agreed-upon construction plans. Change order management is a critical aspect of any construction job, as these wrinkles are costly, in terms of both your time and budget. Some subcontractors even bid jobs at break-even prices in order to get the work, figuring that numerous change orders will provide the profits. To save yourself, make sure your plans are fully detailed. And when compiling line items that subcontractors will be bidding on, be as explicit as possible—for instance, rather than specifying restoration of all woodwork, map out exactly which woodwork as well as which products are to be used. And if such details are not your thing, it's worth paying for the construction management services of an architect.

You and your team will benefit if you follow these guidelines:

❶ Choose your contractor wisely. He is the conductor of your train and the person most responsible for keeping it on track.

❷ Work out a timetable. Make sure you have a detailed construction schedule that everyone agrees upon.

❸ Don't start until you're ready. Changes made during construction are costly and time-consuming. Keep this in mind if the contractor wants to begin without finished drawings.

❹ Maintain accountability. Designate someone, such as your contractor, to track progress and update the schedule regularly.

❺ Pay your invoices on time. Keeping the money flowing keeps everybody working. But hold back some cash before the job's completion (20 percent is a good ballpark figure). If you fail to do this, you'll have little leverage when there are loose ends to be tied up.

❻ Stay in the loop. Schedule regular meetings with your contractor and architect during construction.

❼ Research the lead times for products. Temporarily out-of-stock items can take months to be available. And don't expect anything from Europe to arrive during holidays or the entire month of August.

❽ Learn the rules. If you're in an apartment, make sure you know about the approvals and procedures in your building. And be sure to tip the service elevator guy.

❾ Remember the golden rule. Treat all your subcontractors as valued employees. A morning cup of coffee or an afternoon platter of cookies can go a long way.

❿ Learn to say "Yes" rather than "Let me think about it." All projects require that many decisions be made during construction; being quick and decisive helps keep a project on schedule.

PRO TIP

Chain of Command

Direct your questions or concerns to the general contractor or the architect. Never give direction to a subcontractor. At the beginning of construction, establish a regular time and day for site visits. This will help the contractor to efficiently organize his schedule and questions for you. If you visit too frequently, you'll take his time away from the needs of his crew and slow down construction.

KATHERINE SCHWERTNER, architect,
BAR Architects, San Francisco

A REMODELING TIMELINE

Basic benchmarks to follow when planning the timeline for your remodel:

	500-square-foot addition	3,000-square-foot house renovation
Design and planning	2 months	6–12 months
Permitting	1 month	2 months
Bidding and construction	5 months	12 months
Total	8 months	20–26 months

PRO TIP

How to Be a Good Client

The best clients trust the professionals they hire and learn to tune out unsolicited advice from others. They also understand that design is a creative, evolving process and embrace the changes along the way. They appreciate the character that comes from doing things by hand. To them, their home is an emotional investment, not just a financial one.

BEN BISCHOFF, architect,
Made Architecture PLLC, Brooklyn

10

The Punch List

You're (almost) done! Here are a few final things to remember:

Test everything to make sure it works before you expect to use it for the first time.

Wait to do your final paint touch-ups until your boxes are unpacked. That way, you'll be able to cover up the marks of moving in.

Keep all the extra paint, grout, and tile your contractor will be inclined to throw away. It will come in handy for repairs.

Send in your warranty cards and keep product manuals in a file.

Assemble all the contact information for everyone who worked on your project, so you know whom to call when things need fixing. Standard construction contracts include a retainer you keep for a certain period after completion so that defects can be rectified at a later date.

Learn about proper maintenance of your products and finishes.

Make sure you have the required sign-off on all approvals and permits, and hand in all required paperwork to your local building department.

Say thank you to every person who worked on your project.

Resources We Swear By

ANTIQUES AND VINTAGE

Big Daddy's
Los Angeles and San Francisco, CA
bdantiques.com
Prop stylists' and designers' go-to source for early American, European, and Asian exotica, as well as Big Daddy's own lights made from found objects. And big is right: the LA location fills a former soundstage.

Circa Modern
Chicago, IL
circamodern.com
Mint-condition Scandinavian furniture.

Corey Daniels
Kennebunkport, ME
coreydanielsgallery.com
A combination antiques barn and contemporary art gallery filled with *World of Interiors*–worthy vignettes.

Domino Antik
Stockholm, Sweden
dominoantik.se
Purveyors of vintage Scandinavian lighting (including an outstanding stash of Luxus designs), ceramics, and glass, all ready for international shipments.

eBay
ebay.com
Yes, it's still possible to get deals on the world's biggest auction site—shop locally (so you can pick up bulky purchases and avoid shipping costs) *and* use advanced searches to shop internationally (source a design from the country where it was made and you'll likely pay less).

Etsy
etsy.com
A site representing all manner of small purveyors, Etsy began as a digital storefront for crafters but now also hosts vintage dealers (among our favorites: Hindsvik Shop, Solstice Home, Ethanollie, Privet Soviet, and The Sunday Times Market).

1stdibs
1stdibs.com
An umbrella site representing top antiques dealers of every specialty from around the world, including several shops listed here.

Kirk Albert Vintage Furnishings
Seattle, WA
kirkalbert.com
One of the Northwest's best sources for vintage furniture and folk art, as well as lighting made from old parts—all of which owner Kirk Albert classifies as "perfect imperfections."

Lost City Arts
New York, NY
lostcityarts.com
Modernist classics in mint condition (and priced to match), plus a small collection of reproductions.

Modern 50
Adelphi, MD
modern50.com
Deep holdings of twentieth-century designs with an industrial edge; if you're looking for a steel multidrawer apothecary cabinet, this is the place to find it.

Obsolete
Venice, CA
obsoleteinc.com
Choice primitive and country antiques, plus paintings and scientific instruments.

Olde Good Things
Los Angeles, CA; New York, NY; and Scranton, PA
ogtstore.com
Troves of decorative, priced-to-sell farm tables, metal stools, beveled glass mirrors, and vintage hardware.

Rose Uniacke
London, England
roseuniacke.com
Known for melding English coziness with minimalist rigor, British interior designer Rose Uniacke showcases a mix of clean-lined antique, reproduction, and contemporary furniture.

Ruby Beets Old & New
Sag Harbor, NY
rubybeets.com
A Hamptons institution offering a mix of vintage and contemporary furniture (it's the sole U.S. source for traditional English upholstery by George Sherlock), decorative antiques, lighting, and accessories.

Three Potato Four
Philadelphia, PA
threepotatofourshop.com
Well-selected, affordable Americana divided into evocative categories, such as general store, lake house, and shipyard.

V&M

vandm.com

Like 1stdibs, V&M (Vintage and Modern) presents the wares of vetted antiques shops across the country, as well as throughout Europe via partner Deconet.

Wright

Chicago, IL

wright20.com

A combination auction house and online marketplace specializing in modernist designs.

APPLIANCES

Note that some high-end brands, such as Sub-Zero, Wolf, KitchenAid, and GE Monogram, are not available for online purchase if you live more than a specified number of miles from a seller's location. Sales are limited to dealers within defined geographical limits. Refer to each manufacturer's website to find vendors nearest to you.

Abt Electronics

abt.com

A seventy-seven-year-old family-run outfit with a base of repeat customers and a wide range of appliances and electronics.

AJ Madison

Brooklyn, NY

ajmadison.com

Purveyor of Fisher & Paykel, Bertazzoni, Smeg, and other leading appliance brands; also a good source for sinks and faucets as well as vacuum cleaners.

Ira Woods

Owensboro, KY

irawoods.com

An established family-owned business selling appliances and hardware, including sinks, faucets, shower parts, and toilets by top makers, such as Duravit and Grohe.

Plessers Appliance

Babylon, NY

plessers.com

Wolf, Sub-Zero, Viking, Liebherr, Bertazzoni, and GE Monogram top Plessers' bestseller list.

US Appliance

us-appliance.com

High-end electronics and appliances, including a deep selection of built-in microwaves, plus outdoor grills.

ARCHITECTURAL SALVAGE

Madeira Furniture

Van Nuys, CA (by appointment)

madeirafurniture.net

Reclaimed lumber specialists focusing on rare woods from Brazil.

Ohmega Salvage

Berkeley, CA

ohmegasalvage.com

A decades-old Bay Area supplier of materials for restoring and reviving houses. Its homespun site has info on how to buy a used door, paint a tub exterior, and install a plaster medallion.

Retrouvius

London, England

retrouvius.com

London's premier salvage showroom, run by a husband-and-wife team of celebrated interior designers.

Urban Archaeology

Boston, MA; Bridgehampton and New York, NY; and Chicago, IL

urbanarchaeology.com

A pioneer in the architectural salvage movement. In addition to selling art deco metal gates and carved neoclassical mantels, Urban Archaeology has its own line of reproduction furniture, marble bathtubs, and bath hardware.

Urban Remains

Chicago, IL

urbanremainschicago.com

Rescued old wooden millwork (such as staircase newel posts), doors, doorknobs, and industrial lighting from a city filled with amazing architectural remnants.

BED AND BATH

Brahms Mount

Freeport and Hallowell, ME

brahmsmount.com

Classic herringbone-patterned blankets woven in cotton, linen, or merino wool—the ultimate wedding present.

Coyuchi

New York, NY, and
Point Reyes Station, CA

coyuchi.com

A homespun business solely devoted to organic bedding and bath linens in an understated palette. Its New York location is at ABC Carpet & Home.

Dosa

Los Angeles, CA, and New York, NY

dosainc.com

Dosa's focus is on small-batch fashion, but the brand also produces an extraordinary limited-edition housewares line, handmade often using Dosa's own production remnants.

In Bed with H.D. Buttercup

Los Angeles and San Francisco, CA

hdbuttercup.com/in-bed

All things for the bedroom, including handcrafted mattresses, sheets, and duvet covers from top-drawer small brands.

John Robshaw

New York, NY (by appointment)

johnrobshaw.com

Indian block-printed cotton bedding designed by painter and textile expert John Robshaw and infused with a modern sensibility.

Layla

Brooklyn (by appointment) and
New York, NY
layla-bklyn.com
Owner Alayne Patrick travels
regularly to India to produce bedding,
decorative pillows, and an array of
towels in vibrant patterns exclusively
for her shop. A Layla boutique is
opening soon at New York City's ABC
Carpet & Home.

Matteo

Los Angeles, CA
matteohome.com
Simple, exquisitely detailed bed linens
woven in mills around the world and
sewn in Los Angeles. Matteo has a cult
following among Remodelista readers.

Olatz

New York, NY
olatz.com
Italian linen and Egyptian cotton
sheets (often with monograms and
geometric trim) that look plucked from
a film noir set. All are designed by
Olatz Schnabel and made exclusively
for her store.

Rough Linen

roughlinen.com
Traditionally woven coarse linen
bedding made in Marin, California, by
Australian transplant Tricia Rose (who
gladly takes custom orders).

Serena & Lily

serenaandlily.com
A strong and growing collection of
bedding, fabric, rugs, and window
treatments.

Shop Fog Linen

shop-foglinen.com
Japanese designer Yumiko Sekine's
all-linen towels, bedding, table linens,
and dishcloths.

Swans Island Blankets

Northport, ME
swansislandblankets.com
Investment-piece blankets and throws
hand-loomed in Maine of naturally
dyed wool from local Corriedale sheep.

Tine K Home

tinekhome.com
Danish designer Tine Kjeldsen's robust
collection of quilts, blankets, cushions,
and towels in Nordic patterns.

DECORATIVE ACCESSORIES

ABC Carpet & Home

Delray Beach, FL; Bronx and
New York, NY
abchome.com
What started out as New York's
premier source for rugs has expanded
into an indoor souk offering everything
from lighting to bedding, contemporary
furniture, antiques, clothing, and
jewelry, all with an eco-friendly bent.

Avoca

Locations throughout Ireland
avoca.ie
Ireland's oldest weaving mill, founded
in 1723, offers woolen throws, scarves,
and more at its stores throughout
Ireland. Lunch at one of Avoca's many
cafés will not disappoint.

Badia Design

Los Angeles, CA
badiadesign.com
Moroccan imports: pierced brass
lighting, tajines, tiles, carpets, and
tents.

Ben Pentreath Ltd.

London, England
benpentreath.com/shop
The goods at interior designer Ben
Pentreath's Bloomsbury store extend
from enamelware cream jugs to
Marianna Kennedy's cast resin lamps.
A travel-worthy destination for serious
browsing.

Bloom

Sag Harbor, NY
Owner Mona Nerenberg has an
unerring eye, and her impeccably
styled merchandise encompasses
antiques and newer pieces (including
hard-to-find Italian linens line Society
Limonta).

Canvas

New York, NY
canvashomestore.com
A collection of basics encompassing
ceramics, cutlery, lighting, textiles, and
upholstered furniture made of natural
materials—felt, wood, linen, and, yes,
canvas.

Dunlin

dunlinhome.com
Australian interior designers Nicholas
Barber and Alexandra Bond have
assembled a greatest hits list of
interiors classics, complete with flat-
rate international shipping.

Elsie Green

elsiegreen.com
A Northern California family-run
business devoted to vintage and new
basics, like console tables of reclaimed
pine and fringed linen napkins.

Emery & Cie

Locations throughout Europe
emeryetcie.com
A Brussels-based atelier with a
magical touch. Its output covers the
home front: fanciful metal furniture,
romantic textiles and wallpapers,
hand-forged cutlery, and a range of
tiles, including cement designs.

Folklore

London, England
shopfolklore.com
A refreshing modernist take
on handmade, recycled, and
environmentally friendly design.

Garde

Los Angeles, CA
gardeshop.com
The U.S. source for Van Cronenburg
architectural hardware from Belgium
and other stylishly understated
housewares and accessories that
aren't seen all over.

Greenhouse

Brooklyn, NY
thegreenhouselifestyle.com
Purveyors of eco-friendly wares for
Brooklynites and kindred spirits.

Gump's

San Francisco, CA

gumps.com

San Francisco's answer to Tiffany, Gump's was the first store to sell Edith Heath's ceramics. We're fond of its reissued midcentury furniture line from Walter Lamb.

Jayson Home

Chicago, IL

jaysonhome.com

An emporium of modern and vintage furniture and accessories with an emphasis on solid midwestern comfort.

John Derian

New York, NY, and Provincetown, MA

johnderian.com

A trendsetting shop famous for Derian's plates découpaged with Victoriana and Hugo Guinness's prints of bulldogs and boys' underwear. Also of note: Derian's line of upholstered furniture made by Cisco Brothers and his tree burl shelves.

L'Aviva Home

New York, NY (by appointment)

lavivahome.com

Laura Aviva works with artisan groups around the world commissioning arresting, labor-intensive designs—striped alpaca pillows from the Highlands of Bolivia, felt rugs from Kyrgyzstan—that spotlight age-old craft traditions.

Lekker Home

Boston, MA

lekkerhome.com

Furniture and tablewares with a Dutch and Scandinavian aesthetic.

Liberty of London

London, England

liberty.co.uk

A London style setter since 1875 famous for its floral and paisley fabrics. The department store's home section features goods from U.K. and worldwide designers, many with a dose of British humor.

Lost & Found

Los Angeles, CA

lostandfoundshop.com

Five small storefronts collectively make up Lost & Found, owner Jamie Rosenthal's secretly famous collection of housewares (Spencer Peterman cherrywood bowls, Turkish foutas, grain-sack pillows), as well as fashion and art.

Matter

New York, NY

mattermatters.com

Modern furniture and lighting from eminent designers like Benjamin Hubert, Castor, Jasper Morrison, Faye Toogood, and Piet Boon.

MC & Co.

mcandco.us

A design team's lamps, mirrors, and kokeshi dolls made with great flair. Interior design services are also available.

Merci

Paris, France

merci-merci.com

Reason enough to make a trip to Paris: Merci's charmingly French collection of furniture (vintage and modern), accessories, office supplies, and clothing. All profits go to children's charities around the world.

NK Shop

Los Angeles, CA

nickeykehoe.com

Interior design duo Todd Nickey and Amy Kehoe offer their own furniture designs, as well as a collection of household accessories and European vintage finds with a boho-chic sensibility.

Paxton Gate

Portland, OR, and
San Francisco, CA

paxtongate.com

Skulls and taxidermy mixed in with practical items for home and garden.

Pod Shop

Brookline, MA

shop-pod.com

A tiny gem of a store, Pod is an expertly curated home goods shop with everything from Matteo linens to our favorite Spanish wineglasses.

RE

Corbridge and London, England

re-foundobjects.com

A Northumberland shop with an outpost on the fourth floor of Liberty in London, RE is dedicated to relics and clever recyclings of all sorts. If you're looking for a vintage metal corkscrew, a Chippendale glass jug, or a striped plastic kettle from Senegal, they've got it.

Steven Alan Home Shop

New York, NY

stevenalan.com

The fashion designer now sells the housewares equivalent of his classic American shirtdress.

Tail of the Yak

Berkeley, CA

Our favorite source for paper decorations: garlands, streamers, lanterns, surprise balls, and flowers. Tail of the Yak has no website, but the store at 2632 Ashby Avenue is well worth the pilgrimage.

Ted Muehling

New York, NY

tedmuehling.com

The Brancusi of our day, Ted Muehling makes sculptural jewelry and objects (Nymphenburg Porcelain egg vases, E.R. Butler candlesticks, Lobmeyr carafes and glasses) that are modern museum pieces.

Toast

London, England

toast.co.uk

A British chain that sells men's and women's clothing as well as timelessly understated housewares, from white Turkish cotton towels edged with knotted fringe to wicker log baskets.

Good news: Toast offers shipping to the United States in two to six working days for a flat fee of £20.

Totokaelo Art-Object

Seattle, WA

art-object.totokaelo.com

A collection of totemic objects—Lindsey Adelman's bubble chandeliers, Michele Quan's temple bells, Alma Allen's wooden stools—gathered by Jill Wenger, owner of Seattle's inimitable fashion emporium Totokaelo.

Workshop

San Francisco, CA

workshop-sf.com

Clothing mixed with an eclectic collection of home goods, like indigo-dotted ceramics from Rosalie Wild and Thai pom-pom garlands.

Zinc Details

San Francisco, CA

zincdetails.com

Owners Vasilios and Wendy Kiniris's San Francisco store was one of Remodelista's first Bay Area finds. Committed to enduring, classic design, the architect couple emphasizes European and Scandinavian pieces mixed with Japanese.

FABRICS AND TEXTILES

Anta

Edinburgh, Scotland

anta.co.uk

The ultimate shop for all things plaid and tartan. Anta's fabrics and accessories, including rugs, stoneware, pillows, blankets, and furniture, all hail from Scotland.

Ian Mankin

London, England

ianmankin.co.uk

The British patriarch of ticking, Ian Mankin stocks a wide range of striped (as well as natural) cotton, linen, and velvet fabrics.

Les Indiennes

lesindiennes.com

Hand-blocked monotone Indian patterns printed on cream-colored cotton, available by the yard or as bedding, table linens, and wallpaper.

Les Toiles du Soleil

New York, NY

lestoilesdusoleilnyc.com

Classic French Catalan striped fabrics and goods made from them, including wooden deck chairs with sling seats. Les Toiles du Soleil textiles are upholstery weight and some are weatherproof.

Libeco Home

Meulebeke, Belgium, and Tokyo, Japan

libecohomestores.com

The ultimate source for linen, available by the yard as well as sewn into table linens, aprons, and bedding in an extensive range of muted colors, all direct from Belgium.

Maharam

maharam.com

Textile and wallpaper specialists newly owned by Herman Miller. Geared to architects and designers, Maharam's offerings range from Charles and Ray Eames circles to Paul Smith stripes.

Marimekko

Locations worldwide

marimekko.com

Bright patterns from this perennial favorite can be purchased by the yard (in regular and upholstery weight) and sewn to your specifications at the Manhattan flagship store.

Red Ticking

Seattle, WA

redticking.com

Vintage ticking, table linens, and linen bedding are the main attraction at this Parisian-flea-market-inspired Seattle storefront.

Selvedge Dry Goods

London, England

selvedge-drygoods.org

The retail front of the standout textile magazine, Selvedge sells artisanal fabrics, sewing notions, textile-related books, and a wide range of handmade objects, including Eleanor Pritchard woven blankets.

Virginia Johnson

Toronto, Canada

virginiajohnson.com

Prolific textile designer and illustrator Virginia Johnson applies her bold painterly prints to throws, pillows, scarves, and tunics.

FAUCETS AND FIXTURES

Chicago Faucet Shoppe

chicagofaucetshoppe.com

A great source for classic Chicago faucets for bathrooms and kitchens (including pot fillers), and for Jaclo's Steamvalve Original faucets.

Designer Plumbing

designerplumbing.com

A comprehensive selection of sinks, tubs, toilets, and faucets in a range of prices from American and European manufacturers.

Drummonds

drummonds-uk.com

The British source for classic bathtubs.

eFaucets

efaucets.com

In addition to good customer service and user ratings, eFaucets has one of the largest online offerings of faucets and fixtures for kitchen and bath ranging from Kohler to Vola, American Standard to Grohe, Duravit, and more.

Home and Stone

Brooklyn, NY

homeandstone.com

Authorized U.S. dealer for some of our favorite British brands, like Barber Wilsons and Samuel Heath, as well as top-quality American makes.

Plumber Surplus

plumbersurplus.com

A clearinghouse site for faucets and fixtures that aims to offer the lowest online prices.

Quality Bath

qualitybath.com

A Plumber Surplus competitor that focuses on high-end lines.

The Sink Factory

Berkeley, CA

sinkfactory.com

Specialists in new and vintage traditional plumbing, with a focus on Chicago faucets, which the Sink Factory not only sells but repairs, replates, and customizes.

Vintage Tub & Bath

vintagetub.com

A great source for claw-foot tubs and other reproductions.

Waterworks

waterworks.com

By introducing timeless European styles to the states, Waterworks revolutionized bathroom design. In business since 1978, it continues to lead the way in innovative fixtures, fittings, tiles, and accessories.

FURNITURE MAKERS

Another Country

anothercountry.com

Clear and elegant reinterpretations of farmhouse furniture—three-legged stools, benches, daybeds, and a wall clock—handmade in England of solid oak and other sustainable woods. Another Country was started by Paul de Zwart, the founding publisher of *Wallpaper* magazine.

BDDW

New York, NY

bddw.com

Designer Tyler Hays has attracted a cult following for his finely crafted furniture, which is handmade in a Pennsylvania workshop. The pieces are distinguished by the use of traditional joinery and unusual hardwoods rubbed with natural oils and finishes.

Casamidy

Belgium (by appointment), Brussels, and San Miguel de Allende, Mexico

casamidy.com

Known for its incredible outdoor lanterns, this San Miguel-based design studio also makes opulent metal-framed furniture and other accessories, all handcrafted by local artisans.

Chris Lehrecke

Hudson, NY

chrislehrecke.com

Located on the main shopping street in Hudson, furniture designer Lehrecke's shop features his own modern yet primitive furniture made from locally sourced woods, as well as Ted Muehling's tabletop and hardware designs, mirrors by Maureen Fullam, and Gabriella Kiss's sculptural jewelry.

Cisco Brothers

ciscobrothers.com

This LA-based upholstered furniture maker has shops across the country, including in New York (at ABC Carpet & Home) and San Francisco. Committed to community and sustainability, it uses woods certified by the Forest Stewardship Council (FSC) and water-based glues.

George Smith

Chicago, IL; Los Angeles, CA; and New York, NY

georgesmith.com

Tufted armchairs, Chesterfield sofas, and other comfy upholstered classics made in England—pricey but a lifelong investment.

Iacoli & McAllister

iacolimcallister.com

Rectilinear tables, chairs, and pendant lights, plus a kindred jewelry collection, all by Jamie Iacoli and Brian McAllister.

Koskela

Sydney, Australia

koskela.com.au

A furniture design company whose expansive Sydney showroom is a must-see for anyone interested in Australian modern design. Koskela's tastes are broad, ranging from fluorescent linens and wildly striped rugs to subtle, free-form coat stands.

Newkirk

newkirkny.com

An online gallery showing Scott Newkirk's architectural, church-pew-inspired benches and chairs of ebonized and limed oak—plus art by Newkirk's favorite painters and sculptors.

Ochre

London, England, and New York, NY

ochre.net

The London-based design company that helped shape the current naturalism revival. Ochre makes modern classic furniture and accessories with a palpable warmth. The mercury glass circular table is one of their signature pieces. Canvas (see page 359) is Ochre's sister brand.

Ohio Design

San Francisco, CA

ohiodesign.com

A studio in the Mission District that designs and makes clean-lined furniture from sustainable, chemical-free materials.

Rose Tarlow Melrose House

Los Angeles, CA, and New York, NY

rosetarlow.com

The glam interior designer and antiquarian produces her own furniture, fabrics, and wallpaper with an old-world yet understated flavor.

Sawkille Co.

sawkille.com

A workroom in Rhinebeck, New York, specializing in deceptively simple furniture that references Shaker and other early styles.

Shaker Workshops

Arlington, MA

shakerworkshops.com

This studio aims to reproduce original Shaker furniture as faithfully as possible. Their handmade wooden peg rails are a Remodelista favorite.

GARDEN STORES

Flora Grubb Gardens

San Francisco, CA

floragrubb.com

One of our favorite greenery experts, the aptly named Flora Grubb is an indie landscape designer who helped pioneer the use of air plants in urban settings and vertical succulent gardens (she sells DIY kits). Her Bayview shop doubles as a coffee bar.

The Gardener

Berkeley, Healdsburg, and San Francisco, CA

thegardener.com

Though everything is inspired by the garden, this shop's selection acknowledges that even the most devoted gardener lives indoors. Find plants and pots as well as slippers and rugs here. A collection of large steely gray Yixing pottery is available at the Healdsburg location.

Shovel and Hoe

shovelandhoe.com

Importers of Burgen & Ball tools and other garden gear from around the world, including Japanese garden knives.

Sprout Home

Brooklyn, NY, and Chicago, IL

sprouthome.com

A wide selection of modern planters and terrariums, and a small but stylish collection of outdoor furniture. Both locations offer garden design consultation and floral arrangements.

Terrain

Glen Mills, PA, and Westport, CT

shopterrain.com

An outdoor-living store known for its planters and tools, Terrain also carries indoor furniture and housewares.

HARDWARE STORE GOODS

Liberty Tool

Liberty, ME

libertytoolco.com

A giant cache of antique and used tools, such as wood-handled planes and iron fire pokers.

Machen Supply

Oakland, CA

machensupply.com

Old-fashioned staples like cast-iron skillets and aluminum colanders from a site that specializes in basics for the home, including faucets and chicken coops.

Main Street Supply

mainstsupply.com

A ready source for dinner bells, galvanized buckets (good as wastebaskets), and hand-crank ice cream makers.

KIDS' FURNITURE AND ACCESSORIES

Design Public

designpublic.com

Not just for grown-ups, Design Public offers one of the most comprehensive collections of contemporary children's furniture and décor. And it even has a compelling lineup of dorm gear.

Duc Duc

New York, NY

ducducnyc.com

Contemporary furniture to take you from baby to toddler to preteen; painted finishes and a variety of woods offer lots of options to mix and match. Especially notable for bunk beds and kids' desks.

Dwell Studio

New York, NY

dwellstudio.com

The go-to place for a midcentury-inspired crib; patterned bedding and accessories in a sophisticated palette complete the look. Happily, Dwell has a full collection of adult-size bedding and furniture, too.

Fawn & Forest

fawnandforest.com

From modern furniture standards, such as Spot on Square and Offi, to small-production toys and décor, Fawn & Forest has the goods for the one-of-a-kind nursery.

Modern Seed

modernseed.com

A carefully curated collection of modern goods that take babes and tots from mealtime to bedtime.

Oeuf

oeufnyc.com

Hatched in Brooklyn and one of the first retailers to introduce clean-lined, beautifully made cribs and other kids' furniture to the U.S. market, Oeuf, owned by a husband-and-wife team (he's American, she's French), exemplifies the best in children's design.

Paxton Gate's Curiosities for Kids

San Francisco, CA

paxtongate.com

Located a block away from the original Paxton Gate, this equally eccentric spinoff stocks uncommon vintage toys, classic games, and science kits.

KITCHEN SYSTEMS

Bulthaup

Locations worldwide

bulthaup.com

A forward-thinking German design house that makes luxury modular kitchens that are eminently customizable. Bulthaup has showrooms in thirteen U.S. cities.

Henrybuilt
New York, NY, and Seattle, WA
henrybuilt.com
Henrybuilt makes expertly engineered kitchens using beautiful materials and streamlined designs fabricated in their Seattle workshop. Also check out the company's lower-end line, Viola Park.

Ikea
Locations worldwide
ikea.com
Ikea may have infiltrated every room in the house, but its most notable offerings are its well-designed kitchen systems, which it wisely pairs with affordable, efficient planning assistance.

Plain English
London and Suffolk, England
plainenglishdesign.co.uk
Serene and meticulously detailed English custom kitchens.

KITCHENWARES AND TABLETOP

Bauer Pottery
Los Angeles, CA
bauerpottery.com
This revival of the California ceramics company makes tableware styled after Bauer classics. Bauer also produces Russel Wright's American Modern dinnerware line.

Blackcreek Mercantile & Trading
blackcreekmt.com
Makers of handmade cutting boards with carved handles and cutting board oil that looks as if it was dispensed by a nineteenth-century knifesmith.

Cooking & Tableware
cookingandtableware.com
More than three million products from major manufacturers (including small appliances), and free shipping on orders of $29.99 and up.

David Mellor
Derbyshire and London, England
davidmellordesign.com
Synonymous with genius flatware design. David Mellor's wares are available in the United States from Heath Ceramics. We're also big fans of the work of David's son (and successor in the family business), Corin Mellor.

Didriks
Cambridge, MA
didriks.com
Purveyor of premium kitchen and tableware brands, including Heath Ceramics, Iittala, Simon Pearce, Pillivuyt, and Libeco Home.

Heath Ceramics
Los Angeles, San Francisco (two locations), and Sausalito, CA
heathceramics.com
A resuscitated midcentury California pottery, Heath is best known for its tableware and tiles but has gracefully extended its reach into all areas of the house, collaborating with some of the leading designers of our day along the way. In its retail spaces, Heath frequently sponsors trunk shows and special sales, including Remodelista's Holiday Market.

Huset
huset-shop.com
Brightly patterned contemporary Scandinavian wares, from Swedish dishcloths to Marimekko mugs.

Les Touilleurs
Montreal, Canada
lestouilleurs.com
A high-end kitchen emporium with a demonstration kitchen and an impeccably designed interior by Louise Savoie. Don't miss the beeswax-finished maple spoons and paddles by Quebec artisan Tom Littledeer.

March
San Francisco, CA
marchsf.com
Kitchenwares as couture: in a carefully composed white-tiled boutique, March sells Aga stoves, custom worktables with chunky Carrara marble tops, streamlined terra-cotta wares, and its own spices in chic black containers.

Merchant No. 4
merchant4.com
Modern, sustainable wares, many of them made of wood (such as teak measuring spoons) and sourced from Japan, New Zealand, and Finland.

MetroKitchen
metrokitchen.com
A vast inventory of professional-quality wares for the home chef.

OEN
shop.the189.com
Purveyor of exquisite Asian tabletop goods. Owner Mark Robinson has a knack for sniffing out far-flung ceramicists and woodworkers who usually only sell in their native lands.

Rowen & Wren
rowenandwren.co.uk
A British online store that specializes in sophisticated rustic wares and offers online interior design advice.

Simon Pearce
Mt. Lake Park, MD, and Quechee and Windsor, VT
simonpearce.com
Handmade glassware and pottery. The Belmont dinnerware line in white or celadon is a Remodelista favorite. The restaurant at the Mill in Quechee is well worth a visit.

Sue Fisher King
San Francisco, CA
suefisherking.com
This eponymously named shop stocks table linens from Liberty of London, cutlery from Chambly, and handmade dinnerware from Christiane Perrochon and Lea Ann Roddan.

Whisk

Brooklyn and New York, NY

whisknyc.com

Kitchenwares and tabletop items, from Pyrex measuring cups to Peugeot pepper grinders. A mom-and-pop alternative to the big cookware chains.

KNOBS, PULLS, AND OTHER HARDWARE

Baldwin Hardware

baldwinhardware.com

High-quality door and cabinet hardware, handmade since 1946.

Crown City Hardware

Pasadena, CA

restoration.com

Nickel cabinet knobs, brass doorbells, and other traditional details.

E.R. Butler & Co.

Boston, MA; Milan, Italy; and New York, NY (by appointment)

erbutler.com

The country's most refined custom hardware manufacturer, E.R. Butler specializes in early American, Federal, and Georgian fixtures for doors, windows, and furniture. It also has a firm toehold in the twenty-first century: E.R. Butler makes Ted Muehling's Biedermeier candlesticks and Chris Lehrecke's brass cabinet knobs.

The Hardware Hut

thehardwarehut.com

Knobs and handles of all sorts, including an array of options for custom-paneled refrigerators.

House of Antique Hardware

Portland, OR

houseofantiquehardware.com

Reproduction American door, window, and cabinet hardware; look no further for bronze or brass mail slots with the word *Letters* on the front plate.

Merit Hardware

Warrington, PA

meritmetal.com

Makers of simple brass hardware, from screen-door knobs to floor registers, since 1876.

Nobilus

nobilusluxury.com

Top-of-the-line doorknobs, window latches, and other hardware in craftsman and contemporary styles.

The Source

Vancouver, Canada

sourceenterprises.bc.ca

Actor Corbin Bernsen, who often films in Vancouver, tipped us off to this shop specializing in what it calls "British heritage hardware."

12th Avenue Iron

12thavenueiron.com

This Seattle metalworking studio fabricates the Tom Kundig Collection of steel cabinet pulls, hooks, rollers, and knobs, and sells the wares online.

LIGHTING AND PARTS

Atelier de Troupe

atelierdetroupe.com

A small Los Angeles outfit that makes early industrial-inspired table lamps and sconces and camp-style furniture.

Brendan Ravenhill

brendanravenhill.com

Young, LA-based designer Brendan Ravenhill is one to watch. We love his Cord Lamp, Cord Chandelier, and bent-metal Octagon Facet Lamp—and the fact that he invented a combination trash can and dustpan (available from West Elm Market).

Circa Antiques

Westport, CT

circaantiques.com

An antiques shop that also sells a high-end line of outdoor and nautical-style lighting in polished chrome and brass.

Commune Design

communedesign.com

Colored porcelain light sockets and stoneware table lamps, among other things, from one of the country's best architecture and design collectives.

David Weeks Studio

davidweeksstudio.com

Trained as a sculptor, David Weeks is known for his custom-crafted modern mobile chandeliers of chrome-plated steel and powder-coated aluminum. His Brooklyn studio also produces standing lamps, sconces, and a small collection of furniture.

Lindsey Adelman

New York, NY

lindseyadelman.com

More fine art than light fixture, Lindsey Adelman's custom handblown glass pendants are investment pieces that have inspired countless copies. Adelman's work continues to evolve and now includes more affordable objets d'art.

Lumens

Sacramento, CA

lumens.com

A lighting emporium with a decidedly modernist bent, featuring lights, fans, and furniture designs from Anglepoise, Blu Dot, David Trubridge, Moooi, and Vitra.

Niche Modern

nichemodern.com

Handblown glass globe pendant lights in warm, smoky hues.

Original BTC

originalBTC.com

British bone-china lighting that is a Remodelista all-time favorite.

Rejuvenation

Berkeley and Los Angeles, CA;
Portland, OR; and Seattle, WA
rejuvenation.com

Reproduction lighting, switch plates, doorknobs, and other house parts in styles from colonial to midcentury modern. We're fans of the customizable Burnside Light.

Schoolhouse Electric & Supply Co.

New York, NY, and Portland, OR
schoolhouseelectric.com

An invaluable resource for industrial- and vintage-style lighting and lighting parts of all sorts (including lightbulbs), Schoolhouse Electric now also sells furniture, bedding, tableware, and home-office goods—all well-selected and well-priced. And if you're looking for kitchen knobs and pulls, Schoolhouse Electric has those, too.

Sundial Wire

sundialwire.com

Cloth-covered wire electrical cording in a dazzling range of colors.

Workstead

workstead.com

The founders of the Brooklyn architecture firm Workstead have been leaving their signature around the world in the form of illuminations that pay homage to industrial and mid-century classics.

Y Lighting

ylighting.com

A giant inventory of modern and contemporary lighting designs by Tom Dixon, Artemide, George Nelson, and many others.

MODERNIST FURNITURE AND HOUSEHOLD GOODS

A + R Store

Los Angeles and Venice, CA
aplusrstore.com

Modern pop art and design from around the globe.

AllModern

allmodern.com

A digital department store of contemporary designs. If you already know what you're after (a Vipp trash can? Jasper Morrison wooden kitchen spoons for Alessi? an Artek end table?), AllModern is a likely place to find it.

Circa 50

Manchester Center, VT
circa50.com

Get your Eames, Nelson, Risom, Noguchi, Bertoia, and Tolomeo reproductions here, as well as butterfly chairs.

The Conran Shop

London, England
conranshop.co.uk

The standard-bearer of functional, well-made, and eye-opening contemporary design.

Design Public

designpublic.com

A virtual emporium of modernist wares, from Area bedding to Emeco chairs.

Ferm Living

ferm-living.com

A Danish design studio that makes house-shaped cutting boards, tree-branch wallpaper, and other playful, distinctly Scandinavian wares.

Finnish Design Shop

finnishdesignshop.us

A comprehensive selection of Finnish- and other Scandinavian-designed products, from established classics to new pieces by young emerging talents.

Fjørn

Carmel by the Sea, CA
fjorn.com

Online retailer with a brick-and-mortar shop (called Fjørn-by-the-Sea) devoted to Nordic design in dazzling detail, from Iittala glassware to the full range of Iris Hantverk wood-handled scrub brushes and kitchen accessories.

The Future Perfect

Brooklyn and New York, NY, and
San Francisco, CA
thefutureperfect.com

On the vanguard of contemporary design and the only U.S. store to carry furniture by Piet Hein Eek and Studio Ilse, The Future Perfect also helped introduce the world to Lindsey Adelman's lights and candelabra.

Horne

shophorne.com

Porcelain place settings from MUD Australia, cowhide rugs from Yerra, and lamps from Original BTC.

Just Scandinavian

justscandinavian.com

In their online shop, Rajesh Kumar and Ann Ljungberg assemble an ever-changing selection of Scandinavian furniture and accessories, ranging from well-known classics to small manufacturers you probably won't see anywhere else.

Loft Modern

loftmodern.com

Furniture, lighting, and accessories from a wide array of mostly European designers with an eye toward the sleek.

Mjölk

Toronto, Canada
mjolk.ca

A tastemaking young couple's boutique of Scandinavian and Japanese design (and often an inspired convergence of the two). In a world of modernist design stores, Mjölk stands out for its pure vision and can-do spirit.

Muji

Locations worldwide
muji.us

A Japanese housewares empire with shops around the world, including at New York's JFK International Airport. Muji is all about simplicity applied to everyday basics: stationery par excellence, cotton bedding, white tableware, and cardboard wastebaskets.

Scandinavian Grace

Shokan, NY

scandinaviangrace.com

Brooklyn retail veteran Fredrik Larsson decamped to the Catskills and opened a 4,500-square-foot shop carrying a wide range of Scandinavian goods, including favorites from Asplund and Stelton as well as newer brands like Zweed and Muuto.

Skandium

London, England (three locations)

skandium.com

The best source for Scandinavian design in the U.K., Skandium has two London shops, an outpost at Selfridges, and a well-developed online store.

Tiina the Store

Amagansett, NY

tiinathestore.com

An extraordinary collection of hard-to-find Scandinavian design classics that came together when fashion stylist Tiina Laakkonen was sourcing goods for her own home. She is the sole purveyor in this country of Finnish wallpaper in midcentury butterfly and bird patterns.

Y Living

yliving.com

Design Within Reach's larger (and less rigorous) online competition carries furniture from Knoll, Anglepoise lights, Tivoli Audio radios, and many points in between.

Zangra.com

zangra.com

A Belgian upstart devoted to selling "well-sourced bits and pieces" of its own design and by others, including porcelain switches, hooks, and knobs; molded plastic chairs in bright colors; vintage phones; and some of the best-looking lighting around.

NATIONAL STORES

Ace Hardware

acehardware.com

An easy first stop for household staples (think galvanized buckets and painters' drop cloths). And thanks to the fact that every Ace is independently owned, the chain maintains a neighborly vibe.

Anthropologie

anthropologie.com

Women's fashion combined with furniture and home accessories (including a far-ranging selection of decorative knobs, patterned bath towels, and wallpapers), all of it with a romantic bent.

CB2

cb2.com

Crate & Barrel's youthful spinoff focuses on well-priced modernist furniture, rugs, and pillows. Bargain staple: CB2's undulating clear-glass Numi candleholders for $4.95 each.

The Container Store

containerstore.com

Good for organizational items like wooden coat hangers; shelf liner made of rubber, paper, or cork; and cardboard storage boxes and magazine files from Swedish company Bigso.

Crate & Barrel

crateandbarrel.com

Founded in Chicago in the 1960s to introduce no-nonsense European design to America, Crate & Barrel holds true to its origins. Especially noteworthy: its Marimekko bedding, towels, and plywood trays (which can often be found on sale at Crate & Barrel's online outlet, accessed via its website).

Design Within Reach

dwr.com

DWR helped set off the midcentury design revival by making Eames, Saarinen, and Knoll classics accessible and relevant to the way we live today.

Home Depot

homedepot.com

The convenience store for inexpensive tools, building materials, paint, and more.

Ikea

ikea.com

Scandinavian household design—from kids' step stools to whole kitchens—priced for all. These days, when clean-lined goods crop up in unexpected places, it's almost always thanks to Ikea.

Lowe's

lowes.com

Home Depot's competition is especially handy for inexpensive lumber and turned wood table legs.

Restoration Hardware

restorationhardware.com

A reliable source for well-made outsized furniture, often modeled after French rustic designs. Restoration Hardware also stocks a range of vintage-style lightbulbs.

Room & Board

roomandboard.com

Based in Minneapolis and akin to Crate & Barrel—a chain specializing in sturdy modernist furniture and lighting, much of it safe reinterpretations of edgier designs. A top seller: Room & Board's many versions of its *Dick Van Dyke Show*–inspired André sofa.

Sur La Table

surlatable.com

Sur La Table offers a broad lineup of kitchenwares. We especially like its pots and pans by Staub and Lodge, Chemex coffeemakers, and Duralex tumblers and stackable bowls (a great bargain wedding present).

West Elm

westelm.com

Affordable, modernist design channeled in rapid response to the latest trends. While West Elm focuses on furniture and lighting, its spinoff

West Elm Market is all about the details, from white enamelware serving spoons to orange garden hoses.

Williams-Sonoma

williams-sonoma.com

We rely on Williams-Sonoma for classic tableware and serving pieces. The cleaning department is a Remodelista standby, and we're fans of Agrarian, the new culinary DIY and gardening line.

THE NEW GENERAL STORE

Alder & Co.

Portland, OR

alderandcoshop.com

A fashion and housewares shop that's at once soulful and high style: Astier de Villatte plates, candles, and notebooks; French linen aprons; and Jess Brown crib quilts.

Ancient Industries

Cornwall, CT

ancientindustries.com

Created by "Remodelista 100" author Megan Wilson, Ancient Industries is an inspired compendium of British and European housewares that have been made the same way for eons.

Atomic Garden

Oakland, CA

atomicgardenoakland.com

Well-made everyday niceties, from wooden twine stands to stainless-steel tiffin containers.

Baileys Home and Garden

Herefordshire, England

baileyshomeandgarden.com

Sally and Mark Bailey are British design gurus who preach brilliantly about the use of natural materials and mixing up the old, the new, and the reclaimed. Their compound consists of a shop, a café in a barn, workrooms, a smithy, and their own home—which puts in appearances in *Handmade Home* and other books by the Baileys.

Beam & Anchor

Portland, OR

beamandanchor.com

An artist collective housed in a converted industrial space with a studio and retail shop that sells Beam & Anchor's own furniture, art, ceramics, apothecary items, and other home goods.

Best Made Company

New York, NY

bestmadeco.com

For manly, outdoorsy design junkies: the ultimate handmade axes, first-aid kits, and Pendleton-manufactured red wool blankets. Best Made's cloth-covered extension cord is a classic.

Bitters Co.

Seattle, WA

bittersco.com

A family-owned eclectic general store founded in 1993 and dedicated to well-crafted housewares, many made from recycled materials and of Bitters Co.'s own design.

Brook Farm General Store

Brooklyn, NY

brookfarmgeneralstore.com

Wooden mixing spoons, organic cotton blankets, and satisfyingly simple white dinner plates.

Canoe

Portland, OR

canoeonline.net

A meticulously edited range of items—Anchor matte-black mixing bowls, Eena canvas totes and aprons, Thru Block Shelves—many of which hail from Portland.

Dry Goods

Brooklyn, NY

drygoodsny.com

A great source for affordable gifts that aren't seen all over: Bougies La Française candles, jadeite butter dishes, and the Remodelista-favored El Casco stapler.

Everyday Needs

Auckland, New Zealand

(by appointment)

everyday-needs.com

A star New Zealand stylist's collection of "the pared-back, earthy, and honest."

G. Colton

Los Angeles, CA

gcolton.com

Formerly called Standard Goods, Garrett Colton's Beverly Boulevard shop is modeled after a small-town men's department store—and explains why the goods charmingly veer from striped carpet slippers to coffee beans.

The General Store

San Francisco and Venice, CA

shop-generalstore.com

An astute gathering of new and vintage wares with an emphasis on California-made goods. Get your Studio Patro linens and Luke Bartels live-edge cutting boards here.

Hendy's Home Store

Hastings, England

homestore-hastings.co.uk

In a remarkably restored East Sussex town house, chef and photographer Alastair Hendy mixes a dash of history with a bit of theater—offering old and new utilitarian objects, from bins of candles to farmhouse sinks. On the weekends the shop is also a restaurant, where Hendy serves up simple plates of fresh-off-the-boat seafood.

Hickoree's

Brooklyn, NY

hickorees.com

A Williamsburg trading post stocking Bauer Pottery and striped and gingham bandannas. We're especially fond of their denim aprons and work jackets from Le Laboureur.

JM Drygoods

Austin, TX

jmdrygoods.com

Neighbor to Spartan (see next page), JM Drygoods stocks clothing, hand-embroidered Mexican textiles, and handmade ceramics, as well as Silla, their own line of leather, steel, and wood furniture made in Marfa.

Kaufmann Mercantile

kaufmann-mercantile.com
An online catalog of long-lasting and well-designed goods, complete with background histories. The offerings extend from Silent Glider wooden snowshoes to beeswax tapers to Windmuehlenmesser bread knives.

Kiosk

New York, NY
kioskkiosk.com
A neo-general-store pioneer with a wit and soulfulness all its own, Kiosk presents curated collections of humble goods that it imports from around the world, one country at a time. Its red metal dustpan and horsehair broom are a Remodelista favorite.

Labour and Wait

London, England (two locations)
labourandwait.co.uk
An essential stop in London, Labour and Wait specializes in well-made, timeless household essentials, and has hit upon the nicest toilet brush and receptacle we've ever seen. Its flagship location is on Redchurch Street in Shoreditch, plus there's a store within a store at Comme des Garçons in Dover Street Market. Labour and Wait also has a dozen kiosks in stores throughout Japan.

Le Marché St. George

Vancouver, Canada
marchestgeorge.com
Co-owner Janaki Larsen sells her own ceramics, along with linens from a small family-run mill in Eastern Europe and uncommon Mexican wool blankets.

Manufactum

manufactum.com
Italian and Swiss Navy blankets, French café au lait bowls, German Petromax lanterns—trailblazing German site Manufactum's offerings run far and deep. And there isn't an off note in the bunch.

Objects of Use

Oxford, England
objectsofuse.com
A store devoted to "international archetypes of everyday objects": the Festival of Britain Antelope chair, Japanese knives, Welsh tapestry blankets, and brooms and brushes in all shapes and sizes.

OK Store

Los Angeles, CA
okthestore.com
Teak wastebaskets, Lilith Rockett's white porcelain vases, 1970s orange push-button phones, and one of the choicest selections of modernist flatware. A store that never fails to inspire us.

Old Faithful Shop

Vancouver, Canada
oldfaithfulshop.com
A favorite resource for lighting and linens, as well as enamelware bread bins, tiered-wire produce baskets, and other kitchen basics.

Relish

Portland, OR
shoprelish.com
Goods with a green bent, such as felted wool pillows and wood-framed full-length mirrors.

Spartan

Austin, TX, and
San Francisco, CA
spartan-shop.com
Owner Currie Person has a knack for sleuthing inspirational local designs with subtle southwestern motifs. Her range of not-seen-everywhere ceramics, utensils, and glassware is also available online and in a small San Francisco outpost inside The Voyager Shop.

Tortoise General Store

Venice, CA
tortoisegeneralstore.com
Bonsai scissors, cast-iron rice cookers, teak wastebaskets, and other standout slow-design goods from Japan.

PAINT

Benjamin Moore Paints

benjaminmoore.com
Tried-and-true Benjamin Moore has recently made some breakthroughs. Their new Color Story Collection uses the latest technology to create rich tones by mixing up to eight hues per color. And Benjamin Moore's Aura Paint covers like no other.

Donald Kaufman Color

donaldkaufmancolor.com
Original paint mixologist Donald Kaufman's luminous shades are made to exacting standards and sold by a handful of paint centers across the country. They're worth the splurge.

Eve Ashcraft

eveashcraftstudio.com
Paint whisperer and Remodelista contributor Eve Ashcraft developed Martha Stewart's first paint lines: Aracauna, inspired by hen's eggs, and Everyday Colors. She works as a private palette consultant in New York, but her wisdom is available to all via her book, *The Right Color*, and her line of twenty-eight custom shades for Fine Paints of Europe (see below).

Farrow & Ball

us.farrow-ball.com
The U.K. company synonymous with nuanced colors mixed from long-standing formulations and natural ingredients (that are low and zero VOC), Farrow & Ball also offers a line of historic distemper paints. As a money-saver, people often ask paint stores to copy Farrow & Ball colors, but the results rarely come close.

Fine Paints of Europe

finepaintsofeurope.com
Premium paint formulated for longevity and beauty; color collections include collaborations with the Guggenheim and color expert Eve Ashcraft. Fine Paints of Europe's Dutch Door Kit supplies all the materials for creating a stately entry.

Marston & Langinger

marston-and-langinger.com

After finding that most paints were too toxic for use in its greenhouses, this U.K.-based garden conservatory company launched its own paint collection. Its exterior and interior paints are water-based, non-toxic, non-flammable, and virtually odorless.

Martin Senour Paints

matinsenour.com

In business since 1878, American standard Martin Senour is the master of subtle, layered, and timeless hues, which are perfect for historic and modern homes alike.

Philip's Perfect Colors

San Francisco, CA

philipsperfectcolors.com

Philip Reno, owner of San Francisco's G&R Paint Company (and a Remodelista color guru), makes his own line of 108 full-spectrum colors, all of which have pigments in common, which means that they, as he says, "gravitate towards each other effortlessly."

Pratt & Lambert Paints

prattandlambert.com

All of our paint and color experts are fans of Pratt & Lambert, and that's good enough for us. We're especially fond of architectural color pioneer Donald Kaufman's special collection.

Sydney Harbour Paint Company

sydneyharbourpaints.com

Australian Peter Lewis was inspired to start his business after discovering formulas for Mediterranean paint washes in his grandfather's archives. The company offers a range of water-based wall finishes, from milk paint to mineral paint to lime wash, for an instant rustic look.

Unearthed Paints

unearthedpaints.com

Made from raw ingredients like clay, chalk, marble, and natural pigments, Unearthed Paints are sourced from a German company called Kreidezeit. They're VOC-free, biodegradable, and so green they're vegan. Shades range from ocher, sienna, and umber to ultramarine and spinel.

YOLO Colorhouse

yolocolorhouse.com

Portland, Oregon–based indie company YOLO Colorhouse offers premium no-VOC interior and exterior paints that are available online from Home Depot. Its slogan: "We believe the world can be more colorful and less volatile."

RIBBON AND TRIM

Bell'occhio

San Francisco, CA

bellocchio.com

The world's most inspired collection of what used to be labeled notions: French grosgrain ribbon, Dutch twisted string (and string holders), and green-edged cardboard boxes.

Olive Manna

olivemanna.com

Handmade dry goods (such as colored clothespins) and craft supplies, including linen twine and hand-dyed twill ribbon in Easter egg colors.

VV Rouleaux

London, England

vvrouleaux.com

A showstopping collection of European ribbon and trim.

RUGS AND FLOORING

ABC Carpet & Home

Delray Beach, FL, and Bronx and New York, NY

abccarpet.com

One-stop shopping for every variety of rug—antique, contemporary, dhurries, shag, wall-to-wall, you name it.

Dinesen

Copenhagen and Jels, Denmark; London, England; and Oslo, Norway

dinesen.com

For the perfectionists: this Denmark-based flooring company makes custom wood floors using unusually wide and long planks in Douglas fir and oak, which are treated with lye and white floor soap for a pale Scandinavian finish.

FLOR

flor.com

A modular floor-covering system that uses carpet squares in a range of colors, textures, and patterns that you assemble to create area rugs or wall-to-wall carpeting.

Forbo

forboflooringna.com

The company that made its mark with Marmoleum, a linoleum-like sheet flooring composed entirely of "biobased" materials (it is largely linseed oil, a natural antimicrobial). Marmoleum is hardwearing and comes in a giant range of colors and patterns.

Heritage Salvage

Petaluma and San Francisco, CA

heritagesalvage.com

Heritage Salvage was early to the salvaged wood business. Its Petaluma showroom is stacked with the remains of old barns, water tanks, warehouses, and other sources from California and beyond. Heritage has become a resource not only for architects and builders but also for DIY-ers looking to fix up their homes.

Luke Irwin Rugs

London, England

lukeirwin.com

Bespoke hand-knotted rugs in stunning designs, ranging from subtle textures to vibrant ikats.

Madeline Weinrib Atelier

New York, NY

madelineweinrib.com

Ethnic-inspired modern dhurries and hand-knotted Tibetan rugs in bold colors and patterns that are sold worldwide. Madeline Weinrib Atelier is located on the 6th floor of ABC Carpet & Home.

Morris Etc
morrisetc.com
A color infusion: bright striped handwoven wool rugs from Peru.

Restoration Timber
New York, NY, and
San Francisco, CA
restorationtimber.com
One of our favorite sources for reclaimed wood, Restoration specializes in wood from old barns, mills, and abandoned schools.

The Rug Company
Locations worldwide
therugcompany.com
Patterned carpets designed by Marni, Neisha Crosland, Vivienne Westwood, Paul Smith, and more, sold in Rug Company showrooms and online.

Timeline Wood
Los Angeles, CA
timelinewood.com
A company that calls itself "the pioneer in the designer wood market," Timeline sells ready-to-install boards with the look of reclaimed lumber, as well as timber that's been treated with a variety of distressed paint finishes. All of its wood is sourced from FSC-certified mills in the United States.

Woodard & Greenstein
New York, NY
woodardweave.com
Humble, classic American woven cotton rugs in stripes and checks that work especially well as hall runners.

SHELVING SYSTEMS

Atlas Industries
atlaseast.com
Finely crafted shelving in solid wood and steel available in a multitude of configurations.

Rakks
rakks.com
Favored by architects and widely used in university settings, the straightforward, well-engineered Rakks system has a no-nonsense appeal.

Vitsœ
vitsoe.com
This infinitely flexible shelving designed by Dieter Rams is a modern classic.

TILE

Ann Sacks
Locations nationwide
annsacks.com
A leading national source for modern surface materials, such as concrete tiles, rectangular glass tiles made from silica sand, and sugar-cube white Thassos marble tiles.

Carocim
Aix-en-Provence, France
carocim.com
A Provençal company that has been making patterned and solid-colored encaustic cement tiles since 1850.

Clé Tile
cletile.com
Of late some of the most interesting floor tiles are being made in Sausalito, California, home to both Heath Ceramics and the new workroom, Clé, which focuses on simple ceramic tiles, artist-designed patterns, and Moroccan encaustic cement tiles.

Fireclay Tile
San Francisco and San Jose, CA
fireclaytile.com
Tile handmade in the United States, with an environmentally sustainable focus. The Debris series contains more than 70 percent recycled material.

Fired Earth
Locations throughout England, Europe, and Asia
firedearth.com
A British powerhouse that began as a maker of terra-cotta and has since branched off into tiles of all sorts, as well as specialty paints, wood floors, and more.

Granada Tile
granadatile.com
Based in Los Angeles, Granada derives its name and inspiration from the historic city of Granada in Nicaragua, where the tiles are manufactured using a centuries-old process: pigmented cement is poured into intricate metal molds, then pressed and left to air-dry. The results are harder wearing and more durable than ceramic tiles.

Heath Ceramics
Los Angeles, San Francisco (two locations), and Sausalito, CA
heathceramics.com
A handmade touch and vast line of glazes and finishes (notably matte) sets Heath apart. You can often find us prowling the Sausalito factory showroom, where ceramic seconds and coveted overstock tiles are sold.

Kismet Tile
kismettile.com
Distinctively modern geometrics fabricated in Morocco, as well as a new line of wallpapers.

Maison Artistry
maisonartistry.com
Perfectly imperfect hand-painted terra-cotta tiles made by a California couple in patterns that look like rows of nailheads, textured burlap, and bold arabesques.

Popham Design
pophamdesign.com
Popham Design employs Moroccan artisans to hand-make cement tiles in an array of designs and colors that combine traditional elements with a

contemporary twist. Almond trees, arches, and donkey cart wheels are all sources of inspiration.

Stone Source

Locations nationwide
stonesource.com

Purveyors of natural and engineered stone slabs and tiles (as well as ceramic tile), Stone Source also sells a large selection of refinished reclaimed wood for walls and floors.

WALLPAPER

Deborah Bowness

deborahbowness.com

Master of contemporary trompe l'oeil wallpaper (including a pattern that looks like old subway tile), Deborah Bowness produces her designs in a small factory in Yorkshire, England, using a combination of digital printing, silk screen, and hand painting.

Farrow & Ball

us.farrow-ball.com

Updated traditional brocades, stripes, and lattice patterns, printed using Farrow & Ball's paints.

Flavor Paper

Brooklyn, NY
flavorpaper.com

A growing New York operation that pays homage to sixties pop-art patterns. Bespoke designs available.

Fromental

fromental.co.uk

Handmade traditional papers and fabrics from England.

Mineheart

mineheartstore.com

A British studio known for photographic wallpaper that creates instant architectural details—we particularly love the patterns that present a ghostly wall of white books or white-painted Georgian paneling.

Neisha Crosland

neishacrosland.com

Fanciful, art nouveau–esque imagery from one of London's most talented interiors specialists.

Piet Hein Eek

Eindhoven, Netherlands
pietheineek.nl/en/shop

The influential Dutch designer led the trompe-l'oeil wall coverings trend with his scrapwood papers, which he sells directly and through a number of retailers worldwide.

Pottok Prints

Los Angeles, CA
pottokprints.com

Playful patterns—such as spouting whales—hand-screened on recyclable paper with water-based inks.

Secondhand Rose

New York, NY
secondhandrose.com

New York's longstanding trove of vintage wallpapers (fully cataloged online).

Timorous Beasties

timorousbeasties.com

The Glasgow studio that introduced wit to wallpaper and fabric design, Timorous Beasties has a way with surreal animal and insect patterns and cheeky takes on toile.

Trove

troveline.com

Artists Randall Buck and Jee Levin of New York–based design house Trove take their wallpaper inspiration from far and wide: Hitchcock's *The Birds,* for instance, and the audience of the Venice opera house, Teatro La Fenice.

The Wallpaper Collective

wallpapercollective.com

An online cache of unusual papers from designers like Turner Pocock Cazalet, Hygge & West, and Piet Hein Eek.

Featured Architects, Designers, and Builders

We tip our hats to the following professionals, who contributed ideas, advice, and in many cases designs featured in the book. For our complete listing of recommended architects and designers around the world, see the Remodelista Architect/Designer Directory at Remodelista.com.

ARCHITECTS AND ARCHITECTURAL DESIGNERS

A + C Architecture + Construction
New York, NY
apluscny.com
Josh Pulver

Abueg Morris Architects
Berkeley, CA
abmoarchitects.com
Marites Abueg

Bagchee Architects
New York, NY
bagcheearchitects.com
Nandini Bagchee

BAR Architects
San Francisco, CA
bararch.com
Adam King
Katherine Schwertner
Will Spurzem
Lisa Victor

Burr & McCallum Architects
Williamstown, MA
burrandmccallum.com
F. Andrus Burr

Buttrick Wong Architects
Oakland, CA
buttrickwong.com
Jerome Buttrick

Cary Bernstein Architect
San Francisco, CA
cbstudio.com
Cary Bernstein

CCS Architecture
New York, NY, and
San Francisco, CA
ccs-architecture.com
Cass Calder Smith

DeForest Architects
Seattle, WA, and
Tahoe City, CA
deforestarchitects.com
John DeForest

District Design
Washington, DC
districtdesign.com
Carmel Greer

Dutton Architects
Los Angeles, CA
duttonarchitects.com
John Dutton

Ensemble Architecture, D.P.C.
Brooklyn, NY
elizabethroberts.com
Elizabeth Roberts

Feldman Architecture
San Francisco, CA
feldmanarchitecture.com
Jonathan Feldman

Fernlund + Logan Architects
New York, NY
fernlundlogan.com
Solveig Fernlund
Neil Logan

Finne Architects
Seattle, WA
finne.com
Nils Finne

Front Studio Architects
New York, NY, and
Pittsburgh, PA
frontstudio.com
Yen Ha

Jennifer Weiss Architecture
San Francisco, CA
jenniferweissarchitecture.com
Jennifer Weiss

Jordan Parnass Digital Architecture
Brooklyn, NY
jpda.net
Darrick Borowski

Julian King Architect
New York, NY
juliankingarchitect.com
Julian King

Kimberly Peck Architect
New York, NY
kimberlypeck.com
Kimberly Peck

Klopf Architecture
San Francisco, CA
klopfarchitecture.com
John Klopf

Leone Design Studio
Brooklyn, NY
leonedesignstudio.com
Jennifer Leone

Lindon Schultz
Los Angeles, CA
213-438-0677
Lindon Schultz

Made Architecture PLLC
Brooklyn, NY
made-nyc.com
Ben Bischoff

Malboeuf Bowie Architecture
Seattle, WA
mb-architecture.com
Tiffany Bowie

Matiz Architecture & Design
New York, NY
mad-nyc.com
Juan Matiz

MRJ Rundell + Associates
London, England
rundellassociates.com
Mike Rundell

Naau Architecture
London, England
naau.co.uk
Rahesh Ram

Oliver Freundlich Design LLC
New York, NY
oliverfreundlich.com
Oliver Freundlich

Openstudio Architects
London, England
openstudioarchitects.com
Jennifer Beningfield

Pfau Long Architecture
San Francisco, CA
pfaulong.com
Peter Pfau

Schwartz and Architecture
San Francisco, CA
schwartzandarchitecture.com
Neal Schwartz

Sheila Narusawa Architects
South Orleans, MA
sheila-narusawa.com
Sheila Narusawa

Shubin + Donaldson Architects
Culver City, Newport Beach, and
Santa Barbara, CA
shubinanddonaldson.com
Mark Hershman
Erik Schonsett

Specht Harpman Architects
Austin, TX
spechtharpman.com
Louise Harpman
Scott Specht

Steven Harris Architects
New York, NY
stevenharrisarchitects.com
Steven Harris

Stiff + Trevillion
London, England
stiffandtrevillion.com
Chris Eaton

Tim Furzer
New York, NY
timfurzer.com
Tim Furzer

Workstead
Brooklyn, NY
workstead.com
Stefanie Brechbuehler
Robert Highsmith

Yamamar Design
San Francisco, CA
yamamardesign.com
David Yama

Zack de Vito Architecture
San Francisco, CA
zackdevito.com
Lise de Vito

INTERIOR DESIGNERS

Amanda Pays Design
Los Angeles, CA
amandapaysdesign.com
Amanda Pays

Curated
New York, NY, and
Santa Monica, CA
curated.com
Delta Wright

DISC Interiors
Los Angeles, CA
discinteriors.com
David John Dick
Krista Schrock

From the Desk of Lola
Los Angeles, CA
thedeskoflola.com
Alexandra Loew

Hamilton Design Associates
New York, NY
hdanyc.com
Ellen Hamilton

Henrybuilt
New York, NY, and Seattle, WA
henrybuilt.com
Scott Hudson

Jamie Bush & Co.
Los Angeles, CA
jamiebush.com
Jamie Bush

Kara Mann Design
Chicago, IL, and New York, NY
karamann.com
Kara Mann

Kriste Michelini Interiors
Alamo, CA
kristemichelini.com
Kriste Michelini

Magness Interiors
Santa Barbara, CA
magnessinteriors.com
Carole Magness

MC & Co.
Brooklyn, NY
mcandco.us
Corinne Gilbert

Michaela Scherrer Interior Design
Pasadena, CA
michaelascherrer.com
Michaela Scherrer

Michelle Burgess Design
Bainbridge Island, WA
michelleburgessdesign.com
Michelle Burgess

Nickey Kehoe
Los Angeles, CA
nickeykehoe.com
Amy Kehoe
Todd Nickey

Nicole Hollis
San Francisco, CA
nicolehollis.com
Nicole Hollis

RR Interiors
New York, NY
rebeccarobertson.me
Marco Pasanella
Rebecca Robertson

Rees Roberts + Partners
New York, NY
reesroberts.com
Lucien Rees Roberts

ScavulloDesign Interiors
San Francisco, CA
scavullodesign.com
Kristin Rowell
Marysia Rybock
Barbara Scavullo

Suzanne Shaker Inc.
New York, NY
212-242-0074
Suzanne Shaker

2Michaels
New York, NY
2michaelsdesign.com
Jayne Michaels
Joan Michaels

BUILDERS

Allwood Construction, Inc.
Redwood City, CA
allwoodconstruction.net
Matt Gomez

Aston Barnes, Inc.
Martinez, CA
astonbarnesinc.com
Mark Barnes

Goodingham Brothers Furniture Designers & Makers
London, England
goodinghambrothers.com
Ben Goodingham
Tim Goodingham

Hutchins & Sons Inc.
Niantic, CT
860-739-9873
Glenn Hutchins

Molofsky Builders, Inc.
Glen Ellen, CA
molofskybuilders.com
Mark Molofsky

Santa Lucia Builders, Ltd.
Salinas, CA
slbltd.com
Rick Aguilar

Tincher Construction
Redwood City, CA
tincherconstruction.com
Rich Tincher

Acknowledgments

We are hugely grateful to the following people, who supplied ideas, hands-on help, research assistance, and even places for us to stay while this book was coming to be.

Our team at Artisan: our editor, Lia Ronnen, for passionately championing our cause and steering us through the publishing process; Michelle Ishay-Cohen, who provided invaluable design work; Bridget Heiking, who assisted with the development and editing; Sibylle Kazeroid, for managing all the copy; and Nancy Murray, for overseeing the book's production. And, of course, our agent, David McCormick, who guided us to Artisan, and Susan Sellers of 2x4 for her graphic design acumen.

Our editors and writers at Remodelista, including Sarah Lonsdale, Christine Chang Hanway, Alexa Hotz, Francesca Connolly, Justine Hand, Stacey Lindsay, Sarah Medford, and Michelle Slatalla of Gardenista, who contributed ideas, projects, editing services, brilliant photo styling (thanks, Alexa and Francesca), and general all-around support. And thanks to Josh Groves, who shepherded the project from conception, keeping us all on course and providing good cheer every step of the way.

Our remodeling chapter reflects the hard work of Meredith Swinehart, who researched and wrote about the agonies and ecstasies of overhauling a house, with input from dozens of architects, designers, and builders.

From the beginning, our friend Megan Wilson of AncientIndustries.com has acted as creative council, Remodelista enthusiast, and general all-around sounding board. Not to mention curating and writing "The Remodelista 100" in her intelligently witty prose.

Our genius photographer, Matthew Williams, flew around the world with his camera, patiently accommodating all our requests to shoot just one more doorknob while turning out some of the most beautiful interiors photos we've seen.

Finally, this book reflects the tireless efforts and vision of writer and project director Margot Guralnick, who took the Remodelista concept and ran with it, acting as location scout and scheduler, stylist finder, and transatlantic phone call maker, and, not least, captured the spirit of Remodelista in her sparkling prose. Working with Francesca Connolly in New York, Margot oversaw the book from start to finish and acted as the architect of the Remodelista vision.

Index

REMODELISTA 100 PHOTOGRAPHY CREDITS

The authors and publisher wish to thank the following for permission to reprint their illustrations in "The Remodelista 100."

Vipp pedal bin: Andres Hviid; Duralex Gigogne tumbler: Duralex USA; Swedish brush and dustpan: Kiosk; Original BTC Hector light: Original BTC; Korbo wire basket: Design Within Reach; Tivoli Audio Model One radio: Tivoli Audio; Heath Ceramics Coupe Line: jefferycross.com; Anglepoise Type75 lamp: Anglepoise; Shaker pegs: Shaker Workshops; Staub cooking pots: Staub USA; Bialetti Moka Express coffeemaker: Bialetti; Weber grill: Weber; Miele vacuum cleaner: Miele USA; French enamel house numbers: Ramsign Limited; Iittala Lempi wineglass: FJØRN Scandinavian; Corin Mellor birch plywood tray: David Mellor Design; Växbo Lin dishcloth: Molly Ingebretsen; IBM clock: Schoolhouse Electric; David Mellor Pride cutlery: David Mellor Design; U.S. mailbox: Gibraltar Mailboxes; Bürstenhaus Redecker copper cloth: Sur La Table; Sori Yanagi teakettle: Gateway Japan; bonsai scissors: Bonsai Outlet; Peterboro picnic basket: Peterboro Basket Co.; Opinel knife: Opinel Sas; Felicity Irons rush table mat: David Mellor Design; Zangra industrial light: Zangra; Steele canvas hamper: Steele Canvas; Chemex coffeemaker:

Chemex; Utensil Family by Jasper Morrison: AllModern; Waiter's Friend corkscrew: Brook Farm General Store; Ferro & Fuoco fireplace tools: LoftModern. com; Riess Aromapot: Christina Hausler; Noguchi Akari lamp: The Isamu Noguchi Foundation and Garden Museum; Emile Henry Urban Pitcher: Emile Henry USA; Lodge cast-iron skillet: Lodge Manufacturing Company; Milton Brook mortar and pestle: Canoe; Schoolhouse Electric Alabax pendant light: Schoolhouse Electric; toilet brush and bucket: Labour and Wait; Fort Standard stone trivet: Elliott Romano; Caravaggio P2 pendant light: YLighting; Muuto Toss Around salad servers: Muuto; Coyuchi organic cotton bed linen: Coyuchi; Sheila Maid Airer Dryer: Nutscene; Holmegaard Minima carafe: FJØRN Scandinavian; Iittala Teema dinnerware: FJØRN Scandinavian; Heath Ceramics Neutra house numbers: Heath Ceramics; John Boos cutting board: John Boos; Otto fan: Stadler Form USA; Peugeot pepper mill: Old Faithful Shop; Alvar Aalto Model 60 stacking stool: Hive; Tolomeo clip lamp: Design Within Reach; beeswax candles: Kaufmann Mercantile; steel wastebasket: Schoolhouse Electric; Ian Mankin Furnishing fabrics: Ian Mankin; Studioilse bench: Hive; kitchen serving set by Jasper Morrison: AllModern;

Jeeves coatrack: Design Within Reach; Norfolk willow log basket: David Mellor Design; Pia Wallén Cross Blanket: Mjölk; Cable Turtle: CableTurtle.com; Fiskars scissors: Fiskars; Sawkille Tremper Rabbit Chair: Sawkille Co.; Ørskov glassware: A+R; Haws watering can: Kaufmann Mercantile; Bamboo ironing board: West Elm; Wüsthof knife: Wüsthof; Ikea Bekväm stepladder: Ikea; Hudson's Bay blanket: Old Faithful Shop; El Casco stapler: Wingtip; Burgon & Ball gardening tools: ShovelandHoe.com; Mason Cash mixing bowls: Pacific Merchants; Josef Hoffmann wine coaster: Neue Galerie; Another Country three-legged stool: Another Country; coir and wire doormat: Wayfair; Puukko knife rack by Uusi: Uusi; Best Made cloth-covered extension cord: Best Made Company; Libeco linen: Libeco Home Stores; Pawleys Island hammock: Pawleys Island Hammocks; Slack dry mop: Kaufmann Mercantile; Old English Sheffield silver cutlery: William Turner; Jacob Bromwell colander: Jacob Bromwell; Burnside light: Rejuvenation; Thomas Hoof toilet roll holder: Thomas Hoof Produktgesellschaft mbH & Co.; sheepskin rug: Mojo; Danforth pewter oil lamp: Canoe; wire flyswatter: Manufactum; enamel soap dish: Kiosk; Weck mold jar: Kaufmann Mercantile.

Remodelista editor in chief Julie Carlson
Writer and project manager Margot Guralnick
Producers Francesca Connolly, Sarah Lonsdale
Stylists Alexa Hotz, Francesca Connolly, Lesley Ford
Research Janet Hall, Justine Hand, Meredith Swinehart
Photo research Jenny Pouech
Remodelista 100 Megan Wilson
Editing Sarah Medford, Michelle Slatalla
Interns Rachel Hutchins, Natasha Hirshfeld

Published by Artisan
A division of Workman Publishing Company, Inc.
225 Varick Street
New York, NY 10014-4381
artisanbooks.com

Published simultaneously in Canada by Thomas Allen & Son, Limited

Library of Congress Cataloging-in-Publication Data

Carlson, Julie.
  Remodelista : a manual for the considered home / Julie Carlson with the editors of Remodelista.
      p. cm.
  Includes index.
  ISBN 978-1-57965-536-5
  1. Interior decoration—Themes, motives. 2. Dwellings—Remodeling. I. Title.
  NK2115.C28 2013
  747—dc23   2013006278

Art direction by Michelle Ishay-Cohen

Printed in China
First printing, October 2013

10 9 8 7 6 5 4 3 2 1